KT-491-224

Molly Travers

Talking with Confidence

CAMBRIDGE

Published by the Press Syndicate of the University of Cambridge
The Pitt Building, Trumpington Street, Cambridge CB2 1RP, UK
40 West 20th Street, New York, NY 10011–4211, USA
10 Stamford Road, Oakleigh, Melbourne 3166, Australia

© Cambridge University Press 1995
First published 1995

Printed in Australia by Australian Print Group

National Library of Australia cataloguing in publication data
Travers, Molly.
   Talking with confidence.
   Includes index
   ISBN 0 521 46917 1 (pbk.).
   1. Communication. 2. Public speaking.
   I. Title.
808.5

Library of Congress cataloguing in publication data
Travers, Molly.
   Talking with confidence/Molly Travers.
      p.   cm.
   Includes index
   Summary: Discusses talking and listening in general, taking part
   in conversations, and formal speaking.
   ISBN 0 521 46917 1
   1. Oral communication–Juvenile literature. [1. Oral
   communication.]   I. Title.
   P95.T73 1995
   302.2'242–dc20

                                95.12602
                                   CIP
                                   AC

A catalogue record for this book is available from the British Library.
ISBN 0 521 46917 1 Paperback

Notice to Teachers

The contents of this book are in the copyright of Cambridge University Press. Unauthorised copying of any of these pages is illegal and detrimental to the interests of the authors.

   For authorised copying within Australia please check that your institution has a licence from Copyright Agency Limited. This permits the copying of small parts of the text, in limited quantities, within the conditions set out in the Licence.

Contents

To the teacher   iv

To the student   v

Acknowledgements   vi

Part I Talking and Listening   1

1   Eyes, hands and voice   2

2   Speaking as a group   15

3   Roles within a group   21

Part II Conversations   29

4   Starting   30

5   Getting along   35

6   Joining in   47

7   Outside school   57

Part III Formal Speaking   59

8   Being heard by the audience   60

9   Interviews   75

10   Speaking on your own   87

11   Meetings and committees   89

12   Forums and panels   96

13   Demonstrations   99

14   Debates   104

15   Reports, seminars, and tutorials   108

16   Technical equipment   116

17   Small public speeches   118

18   Making a speech   124

Further reading   136

Index   137

To the teacher

Everyone needs to be able to speak with confidence. The autocratic and authoritarian workplace is on the way out. Members of work groups and teams must be able to speak up positively, and to listen and respond to the contributions of others. Life is not easy for those who cannot make themselves heard.

This book provides self-contained classroom exercises in speaking, which can also be practised every day using content from many parts of the syllabus.

The contents are arranged so that students work in pairs and very small groups, before they begin the work of *speaking* by themselves in front of a large group. These pair exercises are just as important for teaching *listening* and how to be a helpful *audience*. Some confident speakers are thoughtless listeners, bores or bullies. Some shy speakers are so occupied with their shyness that they don't listen either.

Everyone needs to take part in the early exercises, so they can practise listening as well as speaking. However, teachers may want to take some sections in a different order, especially if time is a problem. *A warning:* in an average group, one in five people will be helped by the less threatening exercises, so it may disadvantage them to take the more demanding activities first where only the most confident students will feel comfortable.

Activities are designed to help speakers build skills and develop confidence by stages:

Stage 1: Pairs taking turns to speak and listen (conversations, interviews).

Stage 2: Whole group speaking together, with no individual focus (chorus work).

Stage 3: Groups of three or four, one speaking, others listening (discussions, demonstrations).

Stage 4: Groups of five to eight, one speaking and others listening (tutorials, demonstrations).

Stage 5: Pairs or groups of three presenting to larger groups (panels, forums, seminars).

Stage 6: Large group with individuals taking turns (meetings, discussions, debates).

Stage 7: Solo speech to large group: short formula speeches (welcome, thanks).

Stage 8: Solo speech to large group: performance (tutorial, demonstration, speech).

The activities themselves are in stages, too, so that one group of exercises may involve several ways of speaking with a group.

The book has three sections. Part I gives general practice in speaking confidently, working in pairs, small groups or as a class. Part II focuses on informal and formal conversation, with interaction in pairs or small groups. Part III gives practice in speaking to larger audiences.

The three parts are self-contained, with exercises graded from safe to challenging. The ideal is to move around from Part I to Part III, but to keep to the order of the exercises within each part. However, certain exercises may be more suitable for certain groups, so teachers are advised to read through an exercise before using it. Some exercises take only a few minutes and could be used daily before work begins, or as a part of other work. Others occupy a full hour. Many involve class work in English and other subjects as content.

Many of the exercises could be repeated, as one might practise piano scales, or tennis or golf shots over and over to achieve mastery. Regular practice is the key to success.

To the student:
Listening and being an audience

This book is about learning to be a confident speaker. Every speaker hopes for a listener. Very seldom do we talk without anyone listening. Often people don't talk when they would like to be talking and really need to be heard.

Being a good listener is as important as being a good speaker. Some good speakers don't listen to others. Some silent people don't listen to others, either.

Learning to be a good audience is as important as learning to be a good speaker. In fact, they go together in several ways. If you listen:
- you get to know the other person
- you learn more
- you don't make mistakes
- you can expect others to listen to you.

Everyone is a learner in this book. You are learning how to speak more confidently in many situations. You are also learning how to help others to speak confidently. This means you must show that you are listening, and that you are willing to help the speaker.

Nervous speakers are very afraid of a hostile audience. They are even more afraid of an audience who laughs *at* them. But all speakers like an audience who laughs *with* them.

So how the audience behaves is very important.

If someone has the courage to try out a difficult speaking task, for the first few times the audience needs to be very positive.

Only when speakers are very skilled can they be expected to deal with difficult audiences. Skilled speakers know how to handle them.

Therefore, as an audience you must keep to the rules—to listen quietly, to make helpful and positive comments, and above all, to applaud after each speech with sensible enthusiasm.

Some tips for learning to listen are:
- Get clear what the topic is.
- Listen for the speaker to tell you what the main points are, especially phrases like, 'My first point …', 'My second point …'.
- Something to look at helps the listener: notes on the chalkboard, the overhead projector, handouts. Pay attention to them.
- Make notes of main points, not minor details.
- Watch the speaker's face.
- Note down questions you'd like to ask, and ask them.
- If you know the subject, you'll take in more. So prepare ahead whenever you have the chance. You'll save yourself a lot of revision and research later on.

Good Listening! And Good Talking!

Acknowledgements

We are grateful to the following for permission to reproduce copyright material.

Examples of actual speech are taken from E. Keller, 'Gambits: Conversational strategy signals', and B. Fraser, 'On apologising', in F. Coulmas (ed.), *Conversational Routine*, Mouton, The Hague, 1981 pp. 93-113, 259-71.

'Soup' by Carl Sandburg, is quoted in full, from *Vocies: Anthology of Poetry and Pictures*, 3rd Book, G. Summerfield (ed.), Penguin Books, Harmondsworth, 1968, p. 58.

Ideas for debating are taken from L. Knowles, *Encouraging Talk*, Methuen, London, 1983, p. 154, and inspiration generally from E.J. Burton, *Teaching English Through Self-Expression: A course in speech, mime and drama*, Evans Bros, London, 1949.

Permission to reproduce 'Aussie Rules' by L.D. Gates on p. 15.

Permission to reproduce 'Travellers Need Better Deal: Canadian Expert' by Dugald Jellie on p. 73.

For permission to reproduce photographies and illustrations we would like to thank the following:

The Northern Territory Tourist Commission and General Motors Holden, p. 9; The Age, p. 17; Horizon Photo Library, p. 23; Methodist Ladies' College, p. 24; Otto Rogge/A.N.T. Photo Library, p. 24; Nine Network Australia, p.75; The Age, p. 81; Andrew Chapman Photography, p. 89 ; The Image Bank, p. 22 (photograph taken by Mahaux Photography), p. 91(photograph taken by Kay Chernush) and p. 100 (photograph taken by Gerard Champlong); David Cohen, p. 96.

Every effort has been made to trace and acknowledge copyright but in some cases this has not been possible. Cambridge University Press would welcome any information that would redress this situation.

part one

Talking and Listening

1 Eyes, hands and voice

1.1 Long distance: Eyes

It's difficult to look into someone else's eyes for any length of time. Someone who can 'look you straight in the eye' is sometimes regarded as an honest person, sometimes as a confidence trickster or smooth liar. Children who out-stared adults used to be called 'bold' or 'impudent'. But if they dropped their eyes, they were 'evasive' or proved their guilt by shame! In some cultures, children are expected not to look directly at adults at all. In others, people say to children, 'Look at me when I'm talking to you.'

When you talk to another person, you don't look into their eyes all the time. You look at their mouth and nose, their forehead, or over their shoulder into the distance. The one place you don't look is down. People feel uncomfortable if you drop your eyes, because it suggests one of two things. Either you're unsure and embarrassed. Or you're looking them up and down—and then you embarrass them!

Talking and Listening.
Can you do both at once?

So you usually look at the person you're speaking to for about half the time, and for the rest, you look up and about.

In fact, you can really tell more about a person's feelings by looking at their mouth than you can by looking into their eyes. The eyes don't really hold as much expression.

activity

Mirroring

Mirroring is an old copycat game. Face each other in pairs. One of you is the mirror. Whatever the other does, the mirror must copy. Stay in one place, but you can move your arms. Change turns after a few seconds.

Try this again, but this time keep your arms still, and change only your facial expression. Try showing emotions, such as surprise, sadness, rage, happiness and so on.

Discussion

How long could you keep looking into each other's eyes? Where did you move your gaze to?

Expressions

Stay in the same pairs. This time, hold up both your hands or a sheet of paper so that you can't see each other's mouths. Take it in turns to act out happiness, rage, sadness and so on, using only your facial expression. The other one tries to identify the emotion.

Discussion

Did you know what emotion the other person was trying to show when they had their mouth covered? Perhaps we can't pretend with the expression in our eyes. Do our eyes really tell what we're thinking? In novels, you read, 'He smiled, but his eyes were cold' or 'She laughed gaily, but there was sadness in her eyes.' But can we really read eyes like that?

The direction of the gaze is important too. Often writers tell us *where* a person is looking: 'She stared sadly into the distance'or 'He lowered his eyes guiltily.'

One thing is true. If you start thinking about looking at another person, you both begin to feel self-conscious. The eyes, where they look, and how they look, are a very important part of communicating.

Look deeply into my eyes.

1.2 In the mind's eye: Describing

Can you describe something so well that others can picture it in their own minds? Their picture won't be exactly like yours, of course. Perhaps you have heard about a place and then visited it, and found it's not like you'd imagined? But a good description can help. There's a skill in choosing what to describe and what to leave out. You ask someone what Darwin is like, and they say, 'It's beautiful. It's hot. It's fantastic. It's quite big.' None of that helps you to get a picture. You need details.

My places

Work in pairs, facing each other. Think of a place you know very well. Now picture it in your mind. You can shut your eyes. It could be your house, or a room, or the garden; or a relative's house; or a shop you often go into; or somewhere you've been on holiday. What do you see in your mind's picture? You can include visual facts, events that have happened there regularly or only once, and the people who come there. Now describe this place as clearly as possible.

When you've finished, your partner describes back to you how they pictured the place.

Now the other one describes somewhere they know well.

Our places

Another way of doing this is for both of you to think of one place you both know. One of you begins to describe it (for 30 seconds) and the other carries on from there. You can correct each other while you talk, as the aim here is to get as accurate a description as you can.

Draw and talk

You could do this in pairs or groups of four. Think of a place you liked very much. It could be one you remembered from when you were a child, it could be in your home, or it could be somewhere you went on holiday. Draw the place. It doesn't matter how good your drawing is. You'll find you remember lots of details you thought you'd forgotten. Now take it in turns to describe your picture to the others in the group. What you say is more important than the picture. Drawing jogs your memory.

Conducted tour in the imagination

You are the tour guide. Your partner is a tour group. Take them on a conducted tour (in your imagination) of your own home, or another house you know well, or somewhere you often go, like the supermarket, the shopping plaza or the public library. Give a running commentary on what your 'tour group' is seeing. Your partner can ask questions as if they were a member of a tour group.

Now the other one has a turn as the tour guide.

1.3 Hands, gestures: Non-verbal communication

I don't talk with my hands

Do you wave your hands about when you're talking? Or do you keep them still? Mostly you don't notice whether you do or not. In fact, it's very hard to talk to someone else without moving your hands at all.

But sometimes, especially when you're making a speech your hands get in the way and you don't know what to do with them. In this situation people rub their noses, scratch their heads, pull their ears, bite their nails and fiddle with their pencils.

Often, your hands do the talking, too, when you show how big something is, or which direction it's in. You tell others a lot about how you're feeling by using your hands when you talk. Think of the gestures that show irritation, desperation, or excitement.

Non-verbal communication includes gestures as well as all the other ways that we communicate. You can tell how someone's feeling by the expression on their face, by how they're standing, by what they're wearing, and by their tone of voice. Sometimes you jump to conclusions, but you'll usually be partly right.

Some gestures are obscene or insulting and are intended to cause trouble. They are often used by insecure people who are trying to show strength. These people often like to keep a distance, such as drivers who can escape quickly. Or they are poor talkers, and can only show their feelings by signs. These gestures, including sexist and racist gestures, are inappropriate here and not permitted.

Observing how people use their hands

When you show someone how to do something, you usually use your hands. When you go home, look at how one of your family shows another how to work kitchen equipment, how to cook something, how to fix something in the car engine, how to use some tools, how to work a computer program. Or at school, look at how the science, computer, woodwork or cookery teacher demonstrates a new skill. How much is done with talk, and how much by using the hands to show what has to be done?

Remember the old rule for teaching: tell me and show me, let me try, and then tell me and show me again. This applies to very small children learning to tie their shoelaces right through to skilled scientists and engineers. (Some people, it's true, like to be left alone with written directions to work it out for themselves. But even then, they sometimes get stuck and have to be shown.)

Using your hands to show

Work in pairs, and take it in turns to do the showing.

Each choose a picture from a magazine or child's book. Hold it up so that your partner can see it, and point out what is in the picture. Use one hand to hold the picture and the other to point to each part of the picture you describe.

Use a simple object (pencil sharpener, your watch) to show the other person how it works. Notice how you use your hands.

Think of a task (using a ruler to make a square, folding paper into a paper boat, finding a word in the dictionary) and show the other person how you do it. How much is speech, and how much is done with the hands?

Gestures with meaning or for emphasis

We often use gestures and head movements instead of speaking. These are different from gestures showing something, or expressing emotion. They are sometimes different in different cultures.

Try out these gestures as a group. Suggest other gestures which are used without words, and which are generally understood in Australian culture. Think of any gestures you know which are different in other cultures.

- waving one arm
- raising one arm
- stretching both arms up
- holding out both arms in front (palms down, or up, or side on)
- holding out one arm (palm open, or finger curled, or pointing)
- hand to forehead (palms facing out with hand stiff)
- hand to forehead (with hand curled, palm facing in)
- hand to forehead (with palm horizontal and flat)

- arms folded across the body
- hands on hips (or one hand on the hip)
- hands behind the back
- clapping (fast, or slow; continuously, or twice only).

What do these tell the watcher? Work out as many as you can. How many different meanings do they have? Does it depend partly on the situation, or on what's being said?

You'll probably conclude that it depends on how it's done, who does it, and where they are. The arm, the hand and the fingers all give separate information.

- Waving one arm might be to say goodbye, or to attract attention in a crowd, or to indicate that you're drowning.
- Raising one arm may be to show that you know the answer, or that you want everyone to stop talking and listen, or to salute your leader, or that you're about to hit someone, or to protect yourself from something.
- Stretching both arms up can be yawning, showing religious enthusiasm, or a child wanting to be carried.
- Putting a hand to the forehead may mean you're tired (palm curled out), have a headache (palm flat on forehead), or are shielding your eyes from the sun (palm straight), or saluting an officer (hand stiff), or can't think of an answer (fist on forehead), or you think someone else is stupid (tapping finger).

activity

Observing on your own, and reporting back

On your own: Over the next few days, note as much non-verbal communication as you can outside school, at home or in shops. Include gestures, how people move their heads (nodding, or head on one side, for instance) and the way people stand, how close they stand, and how they sit. Don't include voice pitch or dress.

Which ones give information without any speech?

Which ones tell you how someone is feeling?

Which ones only make sense if they are used to emphasise what someone is saying?

What gestures do you use yourself?

Which gestures are appropriate in some situations and not others?

Make a list, and practise some of the gestures so that you can illustrate them to the group later on.

Reporting back

Work in groups of three or four. Compare your lists and check those that are the same. Prepare a short report for the whole class in which you describe some of the gestures that were used without words, and some used with words. Do not report inappropriate gestures which are unacceptable in the classroom.

Presentation to whole group

One person should read the report, giving time for the other three to demonstrate the gestures. Practise beforehand, so that you make the gestures clearly, and there are no delays.

Are gestures useful for speakers?

Whether you use gestures or not depends on your cultural background, your personality, whether you like to use words rather than signs, your confidence, and where you are and who you're with. Certainly gestures help to attract and hold attention, and when you speak, you're trying to keep a listener's attention. Sometimes they give away how you're feeling when you don't mean to. For instance, there are many ways to sit that show someone else that you're bored or interested.

No gestures

Now finally, work in pairs and tell your partner what you had for lunch. But you must keep your hands and arms quite still—no gestures!

If that was difficult, try this. Tell your partner how to thread a needle or bang in a nail, without using any gestures. Did you manage to keep your hands from moving?

1.4 Something to show: Directions, explanations, descriptions

It's easier to talk if you have something definite to talk about, and even easier if you have something to show your listener.

Here you practise giving clear directions, explanations and descriptions. You'll need to be able to do these things in most jobs.

People often don't give you all the information you need:

- 'Could you hand me that thing?'
  'Which thing?'
  'That thing over there, stupid.'
- 'Can you tell me where the Post Office is?'
  'It's down there and on over there.' He waves an arm.
  'How far down?'
  'Not far. You can't miss it.'

You should work in pairs for all these activities. The whole class can try them out, rather than having one pair demonstrating to the rest of the class. It is important that everyone is taking part, not watching.

Gadget

Work in pairs. Make a collection of gadgets such as staple removers, bean slicers, tweezers, bulldog clips, pliers, or anything with movable parts. You have a gadget each. Sit or stand back to back in pairs, holding the gadget so that your partner can't see it. Describe to your partner everything about the gadget: what it's made of (e.g. steel, plastic), how it looks, what parts move and so on. But don't say its name or what it is used for. Your partner must name it. Then the second person describes their gadget.

Afterwards, you might draw the gadget, label it and write a detailed description of how to use it. This is quite a skill. Often directions that come with products are hard to follow because they're badly written.

Reading maps

Work in pairs. You each have a copy of the same map of a suburb, a town or a region, like the one below. It can be large-scale or small-scale. One of you chooses a point to start and finish, and draws the route in lightly in pencil. Your partner does not write on their map.

Sit back to back so your partner can't see your map. Explain to your partner where to start (e.g. 'in the middle', 'one centimetre from the top left corner'). Then give directions on how to get to the end, using only street or town names and these words: left, right; north, south, east, west; straight on, up, down. Your partner can ask any questions they like, such as, 'Do I go through Horsham?' Change over, so that the other has a turn. They now draw a route on their own map.

If there is little space, you can do this activity sitting side by side, but you shouldn't draw the route on your map. You'll have to remember the route you're directing your partner to take.

If you finish before others, each try out another route. Or write out the directions.

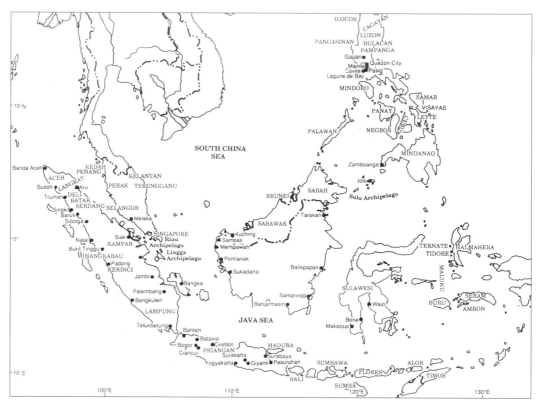

Island Southeast Asia during the nineteenth century.

Identification

Work in pairs. You've arranged to meet someone: a visitor in a café, or a cousin from overseas at the airport. You have to identify each other. Take it in turns to describe what it is about you that makes you different from other people. You should suggest to each other how your description could be made clearer. You're looking at each other, not at yourself, so the other person might be a better judge.

At the end, you can decide to carry something distinguishing as well. But you must describe yourself first.

If you finish before others, write a description of yourself as you can be seen; of course this won't include invisible qualities such as liking horror films or Mozart or KFC.

Drawing conclusions

In pairs, face each other across a table. You each have a small picture of any kind (scenery, pattern, Christmas card, person, cartoon, fashion, machinery, such as the ones below). Don't allow your partner to see your picture.

You describe the picture. Your partner must draw it.

Hold your picture up so that the other cannot see it (as you might hold your cards in a poker game).

Change over, using the other picture.

Discussion

What are the important things to mention when giving directions or describing something to someone? Is it details? Peculiarities? Comparison with something the other knows about? Obvious things?

If you finished more quickly than others, was it because of good descriptions or observant guessing?

Scenery

Machinery

1.5 Voices: How you sound to others

Does your voice sometimes shake when you mean to act tough?

Has your voice ever squeaked when you meant to be serious?

Do you ever sound nervous when you want to sound confident?

Has anyone ever said that you sound rude when you don't mean to be?

Can you really tell when someone is lying to you?

Does your voice express how you really feel?

Sometimes a tone of voice is just habit. And sometimes it's a good idea to change your habits. When we listen to another person, we hear the words—but we also hear how they're spoken.

If someone's voice is monotonous, what they say might sound boring. If it's whining or high-pitched, they might sound weak. If it's loud, they might sound angry. And if their voice is slow, or hesitant, or gabbling, or soft, then they might not be listened to at all.

It's valuable to be able to control your voice, so that it comes out sounding the way you want it to sound, because this can affect how others behave towards you.

For instance, you might want to hide your true feelings. In interviews, you need to sound confident, even if you are nervous. The same goes for making a speech. And it's no good saying something nice in an aggressive voice, or something forceful in a whispering whine. Often we need to be actors.

You need to try out different voices. It's good to have a range to use at different times. If you're trying to make a firm point, you don't want your voice to come out shaky.

If you're used to using one tone of voice most of the time, try these activities to give you a chance to see how many different voices you really have.

If you change your tone of voice, you change the meaning of what you're saying. You also change how other people hear and understand you.

Varying tones of voice

Try out the range of voices you have. It's better to sit in a circle so that people can see each other. You can use two or more small circles to give everyone more turns, and to get people used to varying their voices with a smaller audience.

Look at the list below. A statement is on one side, and a tone of voice on the other.

In turn read each statement, and use the tone of voice beside it. So the first person reads Statement 1, 'Pass me the salt' in Voice Tone 1, a friendly tone of voice.

Statements	Voice Tone
1. Pass me the salt.	1. friendly
2. I need some money for food.	2. sad
3. I've had the job for two years and I want a rise.	3. whining
4. Is anyone serving at this counter?	4. angry
5. Have you marked our papers?	5. pleading
6. Could I speak to the manager, please?	6. flat
7. Would you like some more dessert?	7. cheerful
8. I do like your dress.	8. bored
9. What do you do for a living?	9. violent
10. I'm a clerk in the public service.	10. happy
11. Thanks for the gift. I've always wanted one.	11. welcoming
12. Could you help me with this?	12. soft
13. You owe me $50, don't forget.	13. nervous
14. Don't hit me, you [add a word appropriate to the tone].	14. aggressive
15. Would you like to come to the pictures?	15. shouting
16. Have a good time, then.	16. whispered
17. I'm married.	17. gabbled
18. Would you all please be quiet.	18. hesitant
	19. rude
	20. high-pitched
	21. sarcastic

Notice that there are 18 Statements, but 21 Voice Tones. Start again on the list of Statements, but continue with the Voice Tones to the end before beginning them again. That means Statement 1, 'Pass me the salt', is said in Voice Tone 19, 'rude', and so on.

Keep going round the circle until everyone gets their turn right.

You could also make up other statements and voice tones to add to the list.

Discussion

Someone said, 'It's not what you say. It's how you say it.'

How hard was it for you to vary your voice?

How much was the meaning of the statement changed? How will the listener be affected, and how are they likely to answer? Look at some examples and explain what the meaning really is when the tone of voice is changed.

What kind of person is likely to say, 'Is anyone serving at this counter?' (Statement 4) in an angry voice; in a bored voice; in a hesitant voice? How will the shop assistant be likely to answer each of these?

Answering the tone of voice

For this activity, pairs work well, though the whole class might want to try this out and discuss the results.

Use your imagination to create the context (what is happening when the words are spoken) for the tone of voice you use for some of the Statements 1 to 18.

Using the list on page 10, the first speaker starts with Statement 1 and Voice Tone 1. The second speaker answers in a way that fits in with the tone of voice. For example:

SPEAKER 1 [*jolly*]: Pass me the salt.
SPEAKER 2 [*obliging*]: Yes, of course. There you are.

Then the first speaker changes the tone, and the second speaker answers that.

SPEAKER 1 [*rude*]: Pass me the salt.
SPEAKER 2 [*offended*]: Get it yourself.

You could also give the speaker a character, like this:

LITTLE BOY [*nervous*]: Pass me the salt.
GRANNY [*teasing*]: Don't worry, I'm not going to eat you—or all the salt, either.

We often alter the way we speak to different people. What's right for your best friend mightn't be appropriate for your parents or a teacher. How will it alter the way the words are spoken if the character is:
- male or female
- old or young
- from a different background?

This can be important, because people from different cultures have different conventions about what may be said, and what is rude.

A range of voice tones

Using the list on page 10 again, choose one statement and go round the group, each member taking a different voice tone, in order as numbered. So in turns, you say 'You owe me $50, don't forget' (no. 13) sadly, angrily, pleadingly, etc.

Variation
The first person decides on a voice tone for one of the statements, but doesn't tell the rest of the group what it is. They say the statement aloud. The others have to say what they heard—whether it sounded jolly, angry, flat or nervous to them.

How is the meaning changed when you put the emphasis on different words?
- 'Pass me the *salt*' suggests 'Not the pepper!'
- 'Pass *me* the salt' suggests 'Me—not someone else.'
- 'Pass me the salt!' (angrily) implies 'Wake up, I'm talking to you.'
  And so on.

Meanings in tone of voice

Use the list on page 10 and work in groups.

Try saying some of the Statements in different Voice Tones, and then rephrase the statement so that the real meaning is clearer.

For example, 'I do like your dress,' said sarcastically or ironically may mean something like, 'You look terrible', 'You're overdressed for this party; we're all in jeans', or 'You've borrowed my dress without asking.'

There are times when you intend to mean something different from the words you say, for all sorts of reasons. Sometimes it is more tactful or safer to suggest what you mean, by your tone of voice or your emphasis, rather than saying it outright.

Reading a play

Some plays have been made into films in several versions. Shakespeare's play *Hamlet* has been made into at least ten different films over the years. Laurence Olivier spoke his lines in a quite different way from Mel Gibson, for instance. They made the hero, Hamlet, into quite a different sort of person, even though the words they said were exactly the same. Laurence Olivier was dreamy, while Mel Gibson was full of rage.

The plays here give you a chance to practise a range of tones of voice and emphasis. The first play has three characters, and the second seven characters. This is voice practice, so you can exaggerate the tone.

It's up to your group to decide whether the characters are male or female, or you could make the part suit yourself—if you're a girl, read the part as a female.

My House

Cast: Child, Parent, and Neighbour. Every character has a different tone for each speech.

CHILD [*whining*]: I want a biscuit.
PARENT [*whispered*]: Wait a minute. I'm talking to someone.
NEIGHBOUR [*cheerful*]: It's not teatime yet.
CHILD [*rude*]: I wasn't talking to you.
PARENT [*nervous*]: Sh. Don't be naughty.
NEIGHBOUR [*sarcastic*]: That one's a little darling, I must say.
CHILD [*aggressive*]: Get me a biscuit.
PARENT [*gabbled*]: I'm so sorry. They get tired, don't they? They watch TV so late and you can't get them to bed.
NEIGHBOUR [*flat*]: I think I'd be tired if I had a child like that at home.
CHILD [*shouting*]: Biscuit! I want one now!
PARENT [*hesitant*]: I think—perhaps we'd better—go inside.
NEIGHBOUR [*bored*]: Yes. I've got better things to do, too.
CHILD [*soft*]: I'm a vampire and I'll suck your blood.
PARENT [*jolly*]: Come on! We must go. Lovely talking to you. See you!
NEIGHBOUR [*sad*]: Children have no respect any more.

Now change the words in brackets which describe how the speeches should be spoken. For instance:

CHILD [*angry*]: I want a biscuit.
PARENT [*irritated*]: Wait a minute. I'm talking to someone.
NEIGHBOUR [*nasty*]: It's not teatime yet. (And so on.)

You could try changing the actual words the character speaks, too, and add to the play, simply making up speeches as you go, without writing them down.

The Skateboard Terror!

Cast: postman on bicycle, boy on skateboard, older woman with shopping pusher, boy's mother, man next door, little girl, policeman. Characters maintain the same tone of voice throughout, but change their tone of voice in their last speech.
Scene: on the footpath outside the mother's house.

POSTMAN [*reasonable*]: It was an accident. Can't be helped. These things happen. No harm done.

OLDER WOMAN [*high-pitched, angry*]: No harm done! That's all very well for you. I was nearly pushed over.

BOY'S MOTHER [*tentative, nervous*]: I'm sure he didn't mean it. I hope everyone is all right Are you all right?

BOY [*whispered*]: I'm sorry. I thought he was going to move out of the way.

MAN NEXT DOOR [*loud*]: I saw it all. I called the police.

LITTLE GIRL [*excited*]: He fell down. Postie fell off his bicycle.

POLICEMAN [*authoritative*]: Now what happened? Are you hurt, madam?

POSTMAN [*reasonable*]: I don't think anyone's hurt, officer. Boys will be boys. No-one's fault. One of those things that happen.

OLDER WOMAN [*high-pitched, angry*]: Don't listen to him. He's not the only one involved. I've got a bad leg. And a bad heart. And bad nerves. I've been badly shaken. I've had a shock.

BOY'S MOTHER [*tentative, nervous*]: Oh, dear. Did he run into you? I'm terribly sorry. Where can boys ride their skateboards safely?

BOY [*whispered*]: I didn't mean to run into anyone. I didn't think I'd touched the lady. There isn't anywhere else. There's no ramp in the park.

MAN NEXT DOOR [*loud*]: Officer, I'd like to make a statement. I'm a witness. I'm an impartial bystander. Come over here.

POLICEMAN [*authoritative*]: Thankyou, sir, but I can manage this without your help. Now, is anyone hurt? Is there any damage?

POSTMAN [*changes to rude*]: If this old woman would be quiet, we'd get this sorted out. She was two metres away. If anyone's going to complain, it's me, because the Post Office bike's dented.

OLDER WOMAN [*changes to shaky whining*]: No-one cares about you once you're old. Put you on the scrap heap. Knock you over and kill you.

BOY'S MOTHER [*changes to cheerful*]: You're not dead yet, are you, dear. It seems there's no problem all round. Why don't you all come in and have a cup of tea and some cake? I've just made one.

BOY [*changes to aggressive*]: Don't give them all the cake, Mum. There won't be enough for us. I didn't hurt anyone. Everybody said so. Except her and I don't want her to come in our house.

MAN NEXT DOOR [*changes to pleading, wheedling*]: Does that invitation include me? I don't mind a bit of tea and cake.

POLICEMAN [*resigned*]: Sounds like bribery. I've got to get back to the station. But perhaps I can come in for a minute, just for some cake. Keep quiet, kid, or I'll arrest you for speeding.
[*They follow the mother into her house*]

You might need to practise the plays several times, to get the voice tones right. This will help you to control your voice when you're speaking to people in real situations.

You could keep to the same parts and work at getting them right. Or you could change parts and give everyone an opportunity to practise the whole range.

What effect does the change of tone have on the characterisation of a person—on what kind of personality we think they have?

Writing activities

Adding to the play
Tell what happened when everyone was in the kitchen eating the cake. Remember to add voice tone in brackets after each speech. How will you end the incident?

Giving the characters a past
Write a short character description of each person, showing what kind of background they have. For instance, the postman is reasonable to begin with, and then becomes rude, so what sort of background character would you invent for him? How old is he? What's his personality? Is he short-tempered? Where does he live? What family does he have? How does he behave with his family? What hobbies does he have? How does he get on with others at the post office?

Gender difference
Reread the play, changing the gender of each character. Now you have postwoman, older man, girl's father, girl on skateboard, woman next door, little boy, policewoman. You will have to change the dialogue to suit, substituting 'she' for 'he', 'Dad' for 'Mum', and so on.

How does this change the way you read the parts? More important, how does it change the background character you invent for the postwoman, the policewoman, the father who made the cake? The play's characters in its original form are stereotypes. When you switch gender, do you still have stereotypes?

2 Speaking as a group

2.1 Drama for non-actors: Football

Even if you don't want to be an actor, you do act a part some of the time. You have to pretend to feel confident when you're not, or pleased when you're not, or even angry when you're not. You may have to play the part of student, or teacher, or receptionist, or doctor, or shop assistant, or parent. Each one has a way of behaving that other people come to expect.

If you can't adapt your behaviour to fit different situations, you're at a disadvantage. So there are reasons for using drama for those who don't necessarily want to be actors.

- You can role-play situations you may be in, and drama provides you with words and actions.
- You can get used to an audience while hiding inside a character. Some well-known actors like Laurence Olivier were very shy people.
- You can practise actions in the part you are playing, and you may want to adapt these to real situations.
- You can do things you've wanted to do but haven't felt you could, like shouting or being insulting or hugging people.
- You can find out how it feels to be someone different.

Playing a part

Aussie Rules

by L. D. Gates

Cast: Twelve spectators at a football match: Blues 1–6 and Reds 1–6. The Reds and Blues supporters are seated alternately.

[*Whistle blows. All spectators urge on their teams.*]
BLUES 1: Come on the Blues!
REDS 1: Up the Reds!
BLUES 2: Go get 'em, McKenzie!
REDS 2: Get stuck in, Reds!
[*All the Blues jump up together*]
ALL BLUES: Wow!
[*All the Blues sit down again*]
BLUES 3: What a mark!
REDS 3: That wasn't a mark! He dropped it!
BLUES 4: Shut up!

REDS 4: Wake up, Umpire!

BLUES 5: Good on you, Umpie!

REDS 5: Open your eyes, Umpie!

BLUES 6: McKenzie's shooting for goal!

[*All the Reds jump up together*]

ALL REDS: He's missed it!

[*All the Reds sit down again*]

REDS 6: He's useless!

BLUES 1: What do you know about it?

REDS 1: A bit more than you do, you animal.

BLUES 2: Go get'm, McKenzie.

REDS 2: McKenzie's down!

BLUES 3: He was fouled!

REDS 3: Get up, man! You're not hurt!

BLUES 4: They're carrying him off on a stretcher!

REDS 4: Well done, Reds!

BLUES 5: Umpire! Book that Red. Book that Red!

[*All Blues stand up together*]

ALL BLUES: Up the Blues!

[*All Blues sit down again*]

[*All Reds stand up together*]

ALL REDS: Come on, the Reds!

[*All Reds sit down again*]

BLUES 6: C'mon, Nipper!

REDS 6: Look at Smithie go!

BLUES 1: Stop the mongrel.

REDS 1: Keep going, Smithie!

BLUES 2: Hit 'im! Hit 'im!

REDS 2: Get away from 'im, you ratbag!

BLUES 3: Clobber him!

REDS 4: Awesome, Smithie!

[*All the Reds stand up together*]

ALL REDS: Goal!

[*All the Reds sit down again*]

BLUES 4: Cheats!

REDS 4: What do you mean—cheats?

BLUES 5: He ran too far with the ball.

REDS 5 [*accusingly*]: What about your bloke?

BLUES 6: Who? Nipper?

REDS 6: Yeah. He punched him in the back of the head.

BLUES 1: That was a fair tackle.

REDS 1: Animals!

BLUES 2: Cheats!

REDS 2: Mongrels!

BLUES 3: Poltroons!

REDS 3: What do you mean—poltroons?

BLUES 3: I'm from the Uni.

REDS 4: Aw! Half-wit!

BLUES 4: Scum-buckets!

REDS 5: Garbage!

[*Whistle blows*]

BLUES 5: That's half-time.

REDS 6: Would you like a cup of tea?

Australian rules football

BLUES 6: Thanks.
BLUES 1: Nice game, isn't it?
REDS 1: Most enjoyable.
BLUES 2: How's your Mum getting on?
REDS 2: Don't know. I haven't seen her for a while.
BLUES 3: Where are we going after the match?
REDS 3: There's a good movie on in town.
BLUES 4: How's the kid getting on at school?
REDS 4: Very well. He's got a lovely teacher.
BLUES 5: That helps a lot.
REDS 5: Yes, it's important to teach the right values.
BLUES 6: And teach them a sense of fair play.
REDS 6: I can't stand people who are one-eyed.
[*Whistle blows*]
[*All the Blues and Reds stand up together*]
ALL BLUES AND REDS [*shouting together*]: Kill 'em!!

2.2 Chorus: Speaking all at once

Sometimes you get carried away when you're in a group. Quiet people shout with the crowd and wave their arms at the football, or at the races, or at a rock concert. If it goes too far, as in some demonstrations or football games, the result is mob hysteria or a riot. People who are genuinely against violence can become so involved that they shout abuse and attack others. You feel protected if you're part of a crowd. You aren't protected, of course. Some crowds are dangerous. And it can be dangerous to lose self-control. Look at the play *Aussie Rules* (pages 15-17) for a not very serious example.

In this speaking exercise, you're protected by one other person. All you say in this play is in chorus with another person. Sometimes the whole group speaks at once.

Speaking in chorus

This is a play where every speech is in chorus. Divide the class in half for two groups of 12. If the group has only 10 in it, one person can play both the children and one can play both aunt and uncle, as these parts are the smallest. Every pair speaks their speech together, except where the aunt and uncle and the salespeople have to speak alternately. The salespeople should decide beforehand who will take each speech.

Visitors

Cast: mother and father; their two children, boy and girl; their two teenagers, boy and girl; aunt and uncle; two door-to-door salespeople; the teenagers' boyfriend and girlfriend, Shane and Sharon.
Scene: In the family room.

CHILDREN: Can we go down the street?
PARENTS: It's too late.
TEENAGERS: We're going to a disco.
PARENTS: No! You've got homework to do.
TEENAGERS: We've finished our homework.
PARENTS: No! You're not going out.
TEENAGERS: Please. We said we were going.
PARENTS: Who with?
TEENAGERS: You don't know them.
PARENTS: Who are they?
TEENAGERS: Shane and Sharon.
PARENTS: Well, I don't know.
TEENAGERS: They're really nice.
CHILDREN: Can we go to the shop?
PARENTS: No! It's bedtime.
CHILDREN: We want some sweets.
TEENAGERS: We're ready to go.
PARENTS: I'm not sure.
TEENAGERS: Why not?
PARENTS: We haven't met them.
TEENAGERS: They're coming here.
CHILDREN: Can we see them?
PARENTS and TEENAGERS: No! Go and watch TV.
[*Loud knock at the door*]
TEENAGERS: It's Sharon and Shane!
[TEENAGERS *open door*, UNCLE *and* AUNT *enter*]
PARENTS: It's Uncle and Auntie!
AUNT: Just passing.
UNCLE: Won't stay.
AUNT: Just popped in.

UNCLE: Won't hold you up.

AUNT: Haven't much time.

PARENTS: Hallo! What a surprise!

AUNT: Nothing special.

UNCLE: Mustn't keep you.

AUNT: In a rush.

UNCLE: Must be off.

AUNT: Running late.

UNCLE: Nice to see you.

AUNT and UNCLE [*together, as they leave*]: Goodbye.

PARENTS, TEENAGERS and CHILDREN [*together*]: What did they want?

[*Doorbell rings again*]

TEENAGERS: It's Sharon and Shane!

[TEENAGERS *open door, two* SALESPEOPLE *enter carrying large box together*]

SALESPEOPLE: Can we come in?

PARENTS, TEENAGERS and CHILDREN: Are you selling something?

SALESPEOPLE [*together*]: We're selling [*then alternately*] a special TV box:/Mixed chocolates/dark and milk;/Biscuits/cream-filled/or cheesy;/Chips/chicken-flavoured/or vinegar;/Coke/and Fanta;/Chewing-gum;/Cake/fruit and nut/or chocolate sponge;/and lots more/to last the whole evening/for all the family/at only $40/a special bargain [*together*] just for you.

CHILDREN: Yes! Yes! Yes!

PARENTS: No, thank you. Not tonight.

SALESPEOPLE: Reduced to $30.

CHILDREN: Come on, Mum.

PARENTS: No. It's too expensive.

SALESPEOPLE: $20, your last chance.

TEENAGERS: Where are Shane and Sharon?

CHILDREN: Please! Mum! Dad!

PARENTS: All right. Anything for peace.

[*Mother gives $20, Father takes box*]

SALESPEOPLE: You've got a bargain. See you later.

[SALESPEOPLE *exit*]

PARENTS: I'm worn out.

CHILDREN: Can we have some?

PARENTS: Not now. It's bedtime.

[*Loud knock on door*]

TEENAGERS: It's Shane *and* Sharon!

[TEENAGERS *open door,* SHANE *and* SHARON *enter*]

TEENAGERS, SHANE and SHARON [*all together*]: Hallo!

PARENTS: Introduce us, please.

TEENAGERS: This is Shane and Sharon—Mum and Dad.

PARENTS: Pleased to meet you.

SHANE and SHARON: Hallo everyone.

TEENAGERS: Well, we're both ready.

SHANE and SHARON: Just a minute.

TEENAGERS: Why? What's the holdup?

SHANE and SHARON: Just one thing.

TEENAGERS: What's the matter?

SHANE and SHARON: It's like this.

TEENAGERS: Like what?

SHANE and SHARON: We've changed our minds.

TEENAGERS: Changed your minds?

SHANE and SHARON [*holding hands*]: We're going out together.

TEENAGERS and PARENTS: What!

SHANE and SHARON [*to parents*]: Nice meeting you. [*Backing towards door*] I guess that's it. [*Opening door*] See you later. [*They leave*]

TEENAGERS: I like that!

PARENTS: You're well rid of them.

CHILDREN: Were they your best friends?

TEENAGERS: I didn't like them anyway.

ALL [*together*]: Let's watch TV.

CHILDREN [*grabbing box*]: Let's eat these.

ALL: Yes, let's.

PARENTS [*looking in box*]: Mixed chocolates, dark and milk!

TEENAGERS: Biscuits, cream-filled and cheese!

CHILDREN: Chips, chicken flavoured and vinegar!

TEENAGERS: Coke and Fanta! Chewing-gum!

PARENTS: Cake, fruit and chocolate sponge!

CHILDREN: And lots more!

TEENAGERS: To last the whole evening.

PARENTS: For all the family—at only $20!

ALL [*together*]: What a bargain!

3 Roles within a group

3.1 Power play and positioning

What you say, and the tone of voice you use, both tell others how powerful you feel. Being bossy or assertive doesn't always mean you'll succeed, of course, because the listener may be more than a match, and say, 'Who do you think you are?' Being calmly and firmly polite often gets you what you want far more effectively.

Other things besides your voice also suggest power.

Being bigger and stronger gives primitive power. Big animals eat little ones, unless the little ones learn some cunning during their evolution. A mouse or a bird doesn't have much chance against a cat. But if the mouse can get to its hole, the cat can't fit down it. And the bird can fly.

Who has the most powerful position?

Among humans, we call people cowards who use their physical strength against someone smaller and weaker. If you hit someone, you're called a bully. The same applies if several people attack one person. Nobody admires bullies. Nobody likes them. You may feel sorry for them because they've got problems.

Being tall doesn't make much difference when it comes to choosing leaders. The famous general, Field Marshal Montgomery, was short. So was a well-known early Australian Prime Minister, Billy Hughes.

People in power sometimes dress to make themselves stand out. The tall hats or headdresses worn by bishops, kings, soldiers and witchdoctors add to their height. Public speakers stand while the audience sits. A doctor always asks you to sit down.

Keeping people waiting is a power play. Another way is to get behind a big desk or counter which gives protection, or to sit someone in a lower chair than you. These strategies are usually considered pompous. Confident people don't keep others waiting if they can help it, and they come out from behind their desk to greet you.

Gestures suggest power—for instance, a raised fist, or hands held palm upwards towards the audience to silence them. Taking someone's elbow can be a gesture of friendliness, but sometimes seems more like an arrest.

Standing and sitting

In pairs, face each other, one sitting on a chair and the other standing.

The person sitting asks a favour and tries to be persuasive (e.g. lend me your car, your essay notes, your best jumper, your football, some money). Now try it with the standing person asking the favour.

Change over. Then try it with both standing or both sitting. Repeat the exercise with a different topic.

Try out pleading or friendly gestures, or gestures of resistance or refusal, to match what you are saying.

A preacher in a church pulpit

Reference

Working in pairs, one of you acts the way you normally would, while the other plays the role of an adult you know.

You're asking a family friend to write you a personal reference. Ask the favour, and then tell them what you would like written about yourself. You need to give a confident picture of yourself, without boasting too much.

The friend can agree or refuse. There are many ways of refusing. Try them out.

Change roles, and give the other person a turn.

Discussion

How did it feel to be sitting down while the person speaking to you was standing?

Did the standing person feel more powerful? Or did it depend on which one was asking the favour?

What tone and words were most successful? Or would it depend on who you were talking to (e.g. another student, parent, teacher, employer, family friend)?

Do you naturally use gestures to emphasise your points? Notice the gestures that people around you use, and decide how these gestures add to the meaning of what they're saying.

3.2 One in a group: Family, school, work

Wherever you are, you're going to have to deal with people in groups, and be part of various groups yourself. Individuals behave differently in groups, and groups themselves have a life of their own.

Family

Most people begin their life in a family group. Children, until they can look after themselves, have to be in some kind of group or they wouldn't survive. There are many kinds of family groups, especially nowadays when family life has become more flexible for many people. Four young friends sharing a house can be, in many ways, a family.

Family

In pairs, work out the various roles taken in family groups you know—who leads, who is the peace-maker, who stands back, who disturbs the peace. You'll probably find these roles vary from day to day, depending on the occasion: at meals, on outings such as holidays or picnics, watching television.

Work out a role-play which shows how a typical family group works. Very few people live in 'typical' storybook families nowadays, and they probably never did. Families like that belong to advertisements for margarine!

Can you make a family group work without disagreements or feelings of injustice? Is it possible? What causes disagreements in a family? Why do families meet for celebrations like religious holidays, weddings and funerals, even when some of them don't get on well? The answer is that we all want to belong to groups, and every group is made up of people—with all their faults and strengths.

School or college

You have two kinds of groups at school or college: the class group where members cannot choose each other and have to work together, as in a class or tutorial; and the groups within the class group where people form friendship groups or interest groups.

Methodist Ladies' College 1990

School or college

In groups of three or four, work out what makes a class or tutorial work well.
- What do you mean by 'working well'?
- What differences are there between individuals which will make a good or bad group?
- What about leadership?
- How do different people contribute to the group to make it more, or less, successful?
- How do small friendship groups influence the behaviour or success of the whole group?
- What do you think is the main aim of a class or tutorial group?

Work groups

Family groups change all the time. Parents grow old and children grow up. Individuals change, or leave, or die. New family groups are formed when children marry, and parents become grandparents. We can escape family groups for a good deal of the time, but we know we belong, whatever happens.

School, college and university groups are short-term. The longest you'll spend with any of these is about six years.

But work groups may last for up to forty-five years if you stay in one job. Even if others leave or you change jobs, you have to be able to get on with fellow workers. If you don't talk to your family, or you don't talk to fellow students, that's your decision. At work you have to communicate in order to do your job.

Discussion

What jobs require people to deal with the public all the time?

In what jobs do you have to give directions to other workers, or understand directions given to you?

What jobs mean you can work on your own a good deal of the time?

The jobs people do

Working in pairs, draw up three columns with these headings:
- must deal with people all the time
- deals with people some of the time
- spends a good deal of time working alone.

Write each of the following jobs in the appropriate column.

soldier	potter	judge
receptionist	data processor	tram conductor
doctor	solicitor	secretary
nurse	geologist	waitress
tool maker	scientist	dentist
teacher	engineer	publisher
vet	programmer	opera singer
poet	editor	pop singer
musician	market gardener	tax consultant
actor	salesperson	bartender
electrician	dressmaker	journalist
fashion designer	script writer	psychologist
greengrocer	manager	clerk
accountant	carpenter	TV technician
mechanic	surveyor	plumber
farmer	bricklayer	machinist
tram driver	truck driver	drover
flight steward	checkout person	zoologist
pilot	boxer	footballer
game warden	missionary	film maker

Discussion

Do people always choose the jobs most suited to them?

What decides which job a person will choose?

What makes it difficult to change jobs?

Which of the jobs listed above would suit you best?

Often people don't know what a job involves before they do their training. How can you find out?

You change as you grow older, and a job which seems dull now may turn out to be what you want later on. What is involved in making a major change in your job?

Talk at work

In groups of four, work out tactful but firm ways of doing the following:
* An employer tells a worker that they need to be on time. The worker answers.
* The worker is told that their work is not up to standard (decide what work it is). The worker asks what is wrong. The employer lists all the mistakes. The worker thinks this is not true. What do they say?
* The employer tells the worker that there is no more work available. The employee answers. (Remember to ask for a good reference.)

Discussion

You get the best results if people remain calm and firm, not trying to be rude or funny. Compare in the whole group the various ways the above questions can be dealt with, hearing the words the employer and worker would actually use.

Which do you think are most likely to be successful?

Family, school, social and work groups

Work in pairs. What are the main differences between the four types of groups—family, school, work, social?

Create a character and describe how they would behave in each group (e.g. with the family at breakfast; at college during the day; at a part-time job after school; going out with friends at the weekend). Make the character any age you like, and invent their family, work, education, and social life.

Role-play four short scenes, or write them out.

Discussion

Would your character be a different person in each different situation?

Do some people have several personalities, while others are always the same?

Is it good to adapt, or do you think people are phoney if they change to suit others?

Do people consciously change their behaviour with different people, or is it because different situations bring out other aspects of a single personality?

People are very complicated, and communicating is very complex. That is what makes it all so interesting, but also sometimes rather difficult.

3.3 Who has control? Changing places

Are there some people you have to show respect to? Are there people who have to be polite to you?

Members of a family aren't equal in lots of ways. Their ages are different. Old people are the most respected in some cultures. Some members of a family have more possessions than others. Some have jobs that pay more. Some are bigger and tougher. Some have stronger personalities. In some cultures, women have more power at home, but less power outside. Power changes as children grow up and parents grow old. As parents grow old, they're often glad to let their children take over.

The power or control you have depends on what sort of person you are. But it also depends on who you are and where you are.

The doctor's receptionist has power over the bank manager when she tells him to go to the waiting room. (Notice the sex stereotyping. Did you assume the bank manager was male, and the receptionist was female? Do we assume males normally have power over women?)

The bank manager, whether male or female, has power over the receptionist or the doctor if they want a bank loan.

Who has control?

Post office employees have the power to keep a queue waiting while they sort out something behind the counter.

You, of course, have the power to make a fuss if you're kept waiting by the doctor, the bank manager or a post office employee. Very few people do. Why?

Who tells who?

Work in groups of two or three. How do people in a family ask, or tell, others to do something? How would one member of a family (e.g. parent, sister or brother, or son trying to study) ask another to do something (e.g. go out to get more milk, turn off the television)?

Role-play the sequence, using these examples and others. Concentrate on what people say. Don't move around. Tone of voice and words used are the focus here. Do you have to be more or less careful in what you say with the family than with friends? Why?

It depends where you are

Work in groups of four to six. One of you takes the role of doctor's receptionist. The rest are patients of different types.

How does the receptionist treat old or young patients, smartly dressed or untidily dressed patients, and male or female patients?

A bank manager comes in and tells the receptionist he's in a hurry and must go first. He says that an untidy young man is obviously unemployed and can wait. What does the receptionist say?

How would the receptionist speak to the doctor?

Speak the parts, concentrating on tone of voice. There's no need for actions.

At lunchtime, the receptionist goes to the bank manager to ask for more time to pay back a bank loan. How does she ask?

On the way home, the bank manager has a flat tyre. He has to ask the untidy young man for help in loosening the wheel nuts. How do they speak to each other?

Gender stereotypes have been used in this activity. The doctor and the bank manager could be female. Would that make much difference to how they speak to other people, and how other people speak to them? What if the receptionist were male?

Waiting in the post office

Work in groups of four to six. One of you is a post office clerk behind the counter. It's lunchtime. The rest of you are in a queue. Take on different roles: old lady, young man, businesswoman, housewife, shop assistant (or others you choose). Some of you are in a hurry. Some forget what they want, can't decide, change their minds, ask for lots of information.

How would each person talk? How would they tell other customers, or the post office clerk, to hurry up?

How would the post office employee react to the different people?

Work out what they would say.

Discussion: Stereotypes and power

Did you establish stereotypes for certain people (father, mother, receptionist, old lady, untidy young man, housewife)?

If you did, what were they?

How true are they? Think of people you know.

When you meet people you don't know, do you stereotype them? Do you talk to them to fit in with the stereotype?

Is this fair enough?

Do we, without thinking, talk in a bossier, more assertive way to some people? And talk more politely to others?

Do some people act tough with everyone to show that they don't care who has power?

Should you adapt or change the way you speak to different people?

Could you change *your* position in the power game by speaking in a different way?

part two

Conversations

4 Starting

4.1 Saying hello: People meeting people

What do you say when you meet someone you know well?

When you meet a new person, how you greet them depends on who you both are.

Activity: Greeting new people

In pairs, work out what you'd say (such as: Hi! Hello! How do you do?) when you meet these people for the first time:

- another student
- a friend of your mother or father
- an employer when you walk into an interview
- a council member, when you want to complain about the speed humps
- an electrician who's come to mend something in your house
- someone at a party.

Discussion

What were some of the openings suggested?

Why are some more suitable than others?

Greeting people you know

Now, working in pairs or groups of four, imagine you see the following people unexpectedly in the street, at a club or disco, on the beach, or on holiday.

- your class teacher
- a boy or girl you recognise, and would like to know better
- your boss from your part-time job
- an aunt and cousin
- a person from your class who isn't a close friend
- a close friend with a group of people you don't know.

What sort of opening comments and follow-ups are suitable?

Discussion

You mightn't want to talk to them all, but the mature thing is at least to greet them in passing. How did you deal with this?

In a recent television survey, girls were asked which of these greetings at a party would work:

- 'Haven't I met you somewhere before?'
- 'I bet I can drink you under the table!'
- 'I'm a bit embarrassed asking this, but I'd really like to get to know you.'

The girls said they'd reject all but the third, because it allowed acceptance or a polite refusal.

Do you think it's easier for girls to approach a boy, or a boy to approach a girl? Or is it easiest for girls to get to know other girls, and boys to talk to boys?

What openings did you suggest?
Which do the group think are the best?

4.2 Making conversation: Questions and answers

Do you have trouble making conversation with some people? Maybe they're a different age. Maybe you don't know them well. Maybe you do know them, but you meet in a place where you don't feel comfortable.

Making conversation should be fun, interesting or even funny. It often consists of asking questions and getting answers.

Try out these conversation games. You can give answers that are serious and sensible. Later you could try less serious answers. Take note of the 'conversation stoppers'.

Openers

Work in groups of about six. Sit in a circle. The purpose is to speak clearly and in a friendly conversational way.

The first person asks the person on their right, 'What's your favourite food?' The second person must answer at once. They then ask the next person the same question.

Or they can change the question to, 'What did you do last weekend?' or 'What do you enjoy doing most?' or 'Do you play any sport?'

The answers should be brief, but keep the talk moving. Try to avoid conversation-stoppers, like 'I don't have a favourite food', 'Nothing', and 'No'.

Keeping it going

Work in pairs. You can stay in the circle, sitting side by side, but you'll all be talking at once. One person (the teacher) keeps a record of the time. Imagine you're meeting for the first time. Keep the conversation going for 2 minutes.

You can begin with the same questions as in the activity above, or choose different questions. The other must give an answer that keeps the conversation going.

Change over, so that the other one starts the conversation.

Talking with a group

Work in groups of three or four. Give yourselves numbers 1 to 4. You find yourselves all together at a party, and none of you knows the others.

No. 1 asks a question. No. 2 answers. No. 3 must add to this by asking a further question on the same topic. No. 4 must then join in.

No-one may interrupt if it's not their turn. Continue in turn. The emphasis in this exercise is on every person taking a turn. Often in a group, some people can't get a word in. This time, everyone gets a space and must add something.

Try some of these ways of keeping the conversation going:
- ask a question, e.g. 'And what sport do you play?'
- ask if the other person has done something that you have done, e.g. 'Did you see that TV show last night on Russian rock groups?'
- add your ideas to theirs, e.g. 'Something like that happened to me. It was …'

Practise these and think of others.

Discussion

Did this exercise seem forced and unnatural?

Don't some attempts to make conversation in new situations also seem forced and uncomfortable?

What are the problems?

Who is it easiest to talk to?

Why do we try to make conversation even when we feel a bit uncomfortable?

What are some 'conversation stoppers'?

What are the best ways to keep a conversation going?

Remember that good conversation comes from practising the skills.

You need to listen to the other person so that they can have their say, too. Everyone wants a turn to talk. Some people need to be drawn out, so you can ask them questions.

A few people are natural story-tellers and keep everyone listening. Some people have very interesting things to say.

But if they never draw breath to let others in, they're called bores.

Rude or shy?

Work in pairs. This is more of a challenge. Read through the whole activity before you begin.

The first person wants to start up a conversation. The second person doesn't seem to be interested and discourages without being rude. The first person persists. The second person can decide whether to be won over or not. Try this out.

Change roles. This time the second person is a bit shy and can't think of any way of continuing the conversation. The first person persists, and eventually helps the shy person to have a friendly conversation.

Now the first person tries to make conversation, and the second is rude. Decide whether the first person is rude back, or tries to calm the other one down.

Where are the two speakers looking during these exchanges? What are they doing with their hands? If you don't look at someone, is it a signal you don't want to talk to them? If you do look at someone, it can be friendly—or it can be challenging.

Before you try the activity, read these examples, taking one of the parts each:

At the football

Person 2 doesn't want to become friendly but is polite.

PERSON 1: Are you enjoying the game?

PERSON 2: Oh yes.

PERSON 1: Do you come here often?

PERSON 2: Not really.

PERSON 1: I come every week.

PERSON 2: Mm. [*Looks with concentration at the game*]

On the beach

Person 2 would like to be friendly but is too shy.

PERSON 1: Excuse me, do you have any suntan lotion by any chance?

PERSON 2 [*looking down*]: Yes.

PERSON 1: Do you mind if I borrow some?

PERSON 2: All right. [*Hands it over while looking away*]

PERSON 1: I forgot mine, and I didn't want to get burnt. Thanks for the loan.

PERSON 2: Thanks. [*Looks at the suntan lotion*]

PERSON 1: Do you come here often?

At a concert

Person 2 doesn't want to be friendly, and is rude.

PERSON 1: Did you enjoy that?
PERSON 2: What? [*Looks at* PERSON 1 *all through the conversation*]
PERSON 1: Did you enjoy that piece?
PERSON 2: What's it got to do with you?
PERSON 1: I didn't mean to be …
PERSON 2: Well, would you shut up so I can listen.

Discussion

How did you feel when you were trying to make conversation with an unwilling person?

What happened in your pair? Did the sociable person succeed in having a good conversation with the shy, the unsociable or the rude person?

4.3 Just looking: Meeting someone's eyes

Pair eye to eye

Work in pairs, facing each other. Stand a comfortable distance apart, and make conversation. Imagine you're at a party and have to keep the conversation going.

Look at each other, but allow your gaze to move where it feels comfortable.

Group eye to eye

Vary this by working with the whole group standing in a large circle. Turn to face your partner. You are at a meeting with a lot of people. At the leader's signal, move on to the next person and repeat the exercise.

Discussion

Where do your eyes go when you're talking to another person?

Does this vary with different people you speak to? How?

You get uncomfortable if a speaker stares into your eyes for more than 60 per cent of the time. You don't usually stare into the other person's eyes for long unless you're challenging them, or you're madly in love.

Who has control?

You probably found that you looked at the other person's nose, mouth and chin, even when you were looking into their face. If a person's mouth is covered, it is usually harder to follow what they say. You actually lip-read a lot of the time, especially at a party where there's a lot of noise.

You also glance over their shoulder or at their neck, or sometimes at something you're holding like a pen or a drink.

Sometimes, the speaker looks away. They're likely to be thinking about what they're saying. However, if the listener looks away at someone else, that's usually a sign that the conversation's going to stop.

If you drop your eyes, it's often seen as a sign of weakness or giving in.

Looking someone up and down is an insult.

Looking at the body of someone of the opposite sex while you're talking to them is often classed as sexual harassment, rather than an appreciative compliment. People who want to admire another person's figure usually do their looking when the other person isn't noticing. We're often told that this is male behaviour, but research shows that males and females do this equally.

Eye to eye again

activity

With all this in mind, and working in pairs, try the conversation exercise again. This time sit facing each other instead of standing.

Both try out some of the signals above, whether you're talking or listening, and then discuss how the other reacted.

It's useful to know what signals you're sending, and how others react. You may not mean to be signalling an insult, or a sign of weakness, but that's the message your listener is getting.

5 Getting along

5.1 Tags and hedges: Okay? Orright?

'Okay?' 'orright?' 'you know', 'sort of', 'I mean', 'you see'.

You use these tags and hedges as conversation fillers. They are useful when you want:

- time to think what you're going to say next
- to give others time to take in what you're saying
- to be sure your listener is listening
- to justify yourself
- to change your meaning slightly.

Some people use them all the time, and then they have the opposite effect on the listener. They're irritating.

Read the following out loud, and then reread without the fillers:

- I went to this shop, *you know*, to get a shirt, *you know*. And the shop assistant, *you know*, wouldn't take any notice, *you know*, even though I was first in the queue, *you know*. And I was so angry, *you know*, that if I'd said anything, *you know*, I'd've blown up.
- You take the ball in both hands, *all right?* And you make sure you're holding it firmly, *all right?* You get your balance, *all right?* And then you kick it! *All right?* Simple. Easy. *All right,* you try now.
- It was a *sort of* present, *you know*. And he *sort of* took it, *didn't he, I mean*, that wasn't fair, *was it?* So I clouted him, *you see*. I meant it, *orright?* And I'm not sorry, *okay?*

Discussion

The extra words or fillers ('you know', 'all right', etc.) add to the meaning the listener gets. What exactly do these words mean?

'You know' is added because the speaker needs to justify what they are saying. It's asking for sympathy and understanding. It isn't checking that the listener 'knows'.

'All right' is added as a way of asking the listener if he or she understands, but it can also, in a more subtle way, amount to an order: 'Do this!'

In the last piece, each filler adds a new meaning: Was it really a present? Did he actually take it? Perhaps it was partly fair. He's not sure if he really had good reason to hit him. And he's blustering about not being sorry.

Checking yourself

During the next few days, take note of how often you use these words. Make a list of the different types. Keep a count.

Why do you use them? What do they mean, in context?

Do you use them too often? They might fill in while you work out what to say next, in which case they're useful. Or they might just be a speaking habit.

List any that you hear others use.

Would conversations have less meaning, be less colourful and be harder to listen to, if we got rid of all these fillers, tags and hedges?

5.2 Thanks, praise and blame: Conversational gambits

How many times a day do you say 'please' or 'thanks'? How often do people say it to you? It would be interesting to do a count.

A surprising amount of goodwill in conversations, whether with family and friends or at work, goes with saying 'thank you'.

When did you last get praised for something? When did someone last pay you a compliment? How did you feel?

Sometimes it seems that people are ready to complain about you, or blame you, but they don't bother to tell you when you're doing pretty well.

Even if someone wants to complain about something you did, it makes a difference how they talk to you. If they're angry and rude, you might want to do it again!

It depends how you say 'thank you', too. Sometimes it's sarcastic!

Thanks

Here are several ways of saying thank you (and what they mean):
- 'Thanks for doing the washing up.' (formal)
- 'Thank you very much for doing the washing up.' (more formal)
- 'Oh, you've done the washing up. How nice!' (welcome surprise)
- 'I'm glad you've done the washing up.' (you've done it at last)
- 'It was good of you to wash up.' (not really your job)
- 'Ah, you've washed up.' (you should do it, but I've noticed anyway)
- 'Oh, you shouldn't have done the washing up.' (visitor has done it)
- 'Thanks for washing up!' (sarcastic: you haven't done it)

Thanks and complaint or refusal

Sometimes you're grateful, but need to complain or refuse whatever it is.
- 'Thanks, that's lovely, but I've already got one.' (offer of a present)
- 'Thanks, I'd love to, but I'm going out that night.' (invitation)
- 'Thanks, but we always leave the washing up until morning.' (party)
- 'It's good of you to offer, but I can do it myself.' (offer of unneeded help)
- 'I've enjoyed it, but I won't be able to come again for a while.' (not again)

Refusal when you don't want to offend
- 'Any other time I would.'
- 'I hate to let you down, but ...'
- 'I would normally, but ...'
- 'I don't want to sound mean, but ...'
- 'I like you, but it just wouldn't work ...'

Invitations

Work in pairs or small groups. Practise replying to an invitation where:
- you honestly can't go, but would like to be asked again
- you don't want to go

- you've been once, and don't want to go again
- you've been once and you hope to be asked again.

Role-play what you and the other person say. See if any of the phrases in the lists help you out.

Discussion: Some examples

Read through these lists, and work out when you might use these phrases, or hear other people using them.

Odd apologies—when they're in the wrong

Sometimes, in order to defuse a situation, we apologise to another person when we're really making a complaint.

- 'I'm sorry but I think that's my seat.' (in a theatre or plane)
- 'I'm sorry but you've added up the bill incorrectly.' (café)
- 'Sorry, I didn't quite get that … Sorry, could you speak up a bit … Sorry, the line's bad.' (phone)

When everyone apologises

Sometimes everyone wants to make everyone else feel better, without losing face.

For example, he's forgotten to take her suit to be dry-cleaned, and she needs it for work. She's irritated, and he sets out to clear the air.

HE: I'm terribly sorry about the suit. I was in such a rush, I simply forgot.

SHE: Don't worry. I can wear a dress. It's okay.

HE: Are you sure that's okay?

SHE: Yeah, it'll be better, actually. I'm sorry I got angry.

HE: I did say I'd take it in. I really am sorry about it.

SHE: No, don't worry. I should take my own dry-cleaning in anyway.

HE: It's just that I had that meeting. I'm very sorry.

SHE: Look, I mean it was my fault, I ought to have done it myself. I'm really sorry.

HE: Yeah, I guess it's best if we do our own stuff, with both of us working.

Complaining and blaming

When one person has all the power, they often don't bother to be polite about complaints or blame. Who would say things like these? When is it justified? Do you take more notice if someone gets annoyed?

- 'How many times have I told you to …'
- 'Why didn't you …'
- 'That's a mess, so do it again.'
- 'You always forget …'
- 'Would you mind not doing that?'
- 'If you don't stop doing that, I'll …'
- 'You're doing that just to annoy me.'

Outside observations

Over the next few days, listen to what goes on around you, in and out of school, and make a note of these occasions:

- how people say thank you, and when they don't bother to say thank you
- how people make complaints, and how they can make them less offensive
- how people refuse something, without being insulting
- examples when people don't bother to be polite.

Bring the list to class, where groups can compare their notes.

As well, during the week practise some better ways to say thank you, to make a complaint, to ask for something, and to refuse something. What was the result?

5.3 Smoothing the way: Saying you're sorry

How often do you say 'sorry'?

You probably say it without thinking when you bump someone by mistake.

Do you sometimes know you're wrong, but don't want to admit it?

Has anyone ever refused to accept your apology?

Apologising is mostly a social habit that you hardly notice. Sometimes you mean it when you say 'sorry'; sometimes you don't. Apologies help to keep friendships going.

Apologies mean all sorts of different things, often in quite subtle ways. Learning how to apologise without being too humble is quite an art.

'Apologies are viewed … as one type of remedial work, action taken to change what might be seen as an offensive act into an acceptable one,' Bruce Fraser says.[1]

We smooth our way in relationships with other people by:

- explanations, where we offer an explanation for something misunderstood by another: 'Your brother did say I could borrow it' or 'I thought it was mine' or 'The teacher said we could.'
- requests, where we ask or comment before doing something which might be upsetting to another: 'Excuse me' as we push past, or 'Do you mind if I go ahead?' or 'Is it all right if I take this?'
- apologies, where we have upset or offended someone unintentionally—or intentionally—and want to put it right.

Fraser and Edmondson give some strategies:

Giving an apology

- Formal, after the event: 'I want to apologise for …'; 'I must apologise for …'; 'Let me apologise for …'.
- Less formal, used at the time: 'Please excuse me for …'; 'I beg your pardon'; 'Please forgive me.'
- Informal, used at the time or later: 'I'm terribly sorry for …'; 'I really do regret that …'.
- Informal, admitting fault: 'That was my fault'; 'Sorry. That was a dumb thing to do.'
- Formal, covering future actions: 'I'll make sure it doesn't happen again.'
- Formal, offering compensation: 'Look, I'll get it repaired/pay for the damage/get you a new one.'

There are other cases which are specific without actually saying you're sorry. Or they're given when there's been no offence. But they're part of daily communication to keep people happy.

- 'Was that your foot?' (apology implied)
- 'Excuse me!' (when someone shoves through: more a warning than an apology)
- 'Sorry for being alive!' (sarcasm, not an apology)
- 'How can I ever thank you?' (more gratitude than apology)
- 'I'm sorry you had to wait so long.' (when it isn't the speaker's fault at all)

Answering an apology

When someone apologises, you have to decide how to receive it. That depends how you feel about the offence.

- Accepting an apology: 'It was really my fault'; 'It was partly my fault'; 'Don't worry'; 'Don't mention it'; 'It didn't matter'; 'You couldn't really help it'; 'That's all right'; 'It did upset me a bit.'

---

1 Examples of phrases are taken from Bruce Fraser's paper 'On apologising', and Willis J. Edmondson's paper 'On saying you're sorry', both from *Conversational Routine*, F. Coulmas (ed.), Mouton, The Hague, 1981.

- Refusing to accept an apology: 'So you ought to!'; 'I should think so!'; 'It's no good saying you're sorry. The harm's done'; 'I'm sorry. I cannot accept your apology.'

People refuse to accept an apology when they really want trouble between the two people to continue. Powerful people sometimes refuse to accept an apology from less powerful people: parent and child, or teacher and student, or employer and employee. Even then, a refusal is very unusual, and leads to a bad relationship—and parents, teachers and employers usually don't want bad relationships.

As a result, the person who has apologised often feels very angry and humiliated, and wishes they hadn't apologised. They feel like saying something very rude back. If it's an equal, they often do. If it's someone more powerful, the best answer is, 'I'm sorry you feel like that.' This shows that the person who's apologising is more generous, nicer, and stronger. It's probably the best answer under any circumstances, and can make the person who refused the apology look quite small.

Being sorry

In pairs, work out what you'd say in these situations and how the other person might answer. There'll be several ways of apologising and ways of answering, depending on the circumstances, the relationship, and how people want things to work out in the future. Look at the lists above, and see which phrases fit best. Decide who's to take each part, and act out the scene between you.

- you keep someone waiting
- you want to refuse an invitation
- you take someone else's shopping trolley by mistake
- you break your friend's Walkman
- you want to clear up an argument, which was just as much the other person's fault
- you want to get someone out of a bad mood, though the fault was theirs
- you run over a neighbour's cat.

'Never apologise! Never explain!'

So some people say, because they think that if you admit you're in the wrong, others will take advantage of you. Apologising, so they think, is a sign of weakness.

Certainly, some people apologise when someone else bumps into them. Absent-minded people sometimes say sorry even when they bump into a chair. Some people are so apologetic they seem to be saying, 'I'm sorry I'm alive!'

But playing so tough that you can't ever admit you're wrong is a sign of weakness and low self-confidence. It's usually a brash and defensive way of hiding the fact that you think you're wrong a lot of the time.

Strong and confident people can apologise without losing face. In fact, apologising is more likely to put them in control of the situation by taking responsibility. People who can take responsibility are seen by others to be strong.

Females are said to apologise to males in order to clear the atmosphere, even when the trouble was caused by the male. As one woman said, 'When I say I'm sorry to him, I really mean I'm sorry I every married such a bad-tempered old so-and-so. Or else that I'm sorry for him being such a misery. But he doesn't know that, and it gets him out of his mood.' But some women are prepared to take all the blame: 'It's my fault. I upset him.'

When to apologise and when not to

In pairs, or groups of four, work out a situation with parents, friends, teachers, employers, workmates, where an apology isn't accepted. Give several ways of answering, and decide on the best. Use the list of phrases above if you need them.

Do females apologise too much?

In pairs, or groups of four, work out situations where girls or women might or might not apologise after a disagreement with a male. You could try out these:

(a) his fault and she apologises: how does he answer?

(b) her fault and she apologises: how does he answer?

(c) his fault and she tries to clear the air without apologising: how does he respond?

(d) no-one apologises.

The following incidents are examples. Try them out or think of your own:

- he tells her the wrong time or place, so she's late or misses him
- she already has something he bought for her birthday
- she buys him a wallet but he already has one he likes
- she's half an hour late because she missed the train
- he's half an hour late because he was looking at sports equipment
- he doesn't eat what she's bought for a special dinner
- he's burnt the dinner and it's inedible
- she damages his car
- he damages her car.

When we have to get on with friends, family, schoolmates or workmates, keeping the peace is important. Making sure we get respect is important, too. Saying you're sorry so you and the other person don't lose face, is part of all this.

5.4 I don't know: How to admit ignorance

Do you sometimes feel people will think you're stupid if you don't know the answer?

Is it worth making something up if you don't know? Some people like to be first with the gossip, and exaggerate stories about others.

You'd be surprised how many people, young and old, won't admit they don't know. In a survey, 80 per cent of secondary school students said they were nervous about risking an answer in class because they might be wrong.

Risking an answer is worthwhile. Nobody can know everything!

But sometimes, instead of giving wrong directions to someone, saying you don't know is the only answer.

And sometimes, if you make things up, you get caught out and look twice as silly.

Even if you don't know the answer to the question asked, there are ways of helping, or keeping a conversation going.

You could tell the enquirer where else they could find the answer.

There's a true story of an Australian university student in America who got an exam question which said, 'Write an account of the American education system.' He wrote, 'I don't know anything about it, so I've written an account of the Australian education system.' And he got a very good mark. (It won't always work like that, unfortunately!)

Admitting you don't know

Work in pairs or small groups. You want to help these people, or you want to keep the conversation going. How would you answer the following?

- Someone asks you the way to a place you've never heard of.
- You're asked a question in an interview for a job, and you should know the answer to it, but you don't.
- You're asked at a party if you know who'll win the football finals and you're not interested in football.

How do I say I don't know?

- You're asked your opinion of some economic question in a job interview, and you don't have an opinion.
- The person next to you at a meal in a restaurant asks if you know anything about the opera (or heavy metal bands etc.), and you don't know.

If you don't know, are there occasions when you should make something up? Some people do, rather than admit they don't know.

What if you just said, 'I don't know' and left it at that? That's a sure way of ending the conversation.

Two alternatives are, 'I don't know but …' and you offer something helpful.

Or you ask the other person their views instead.

How would either of these alternatives work with the situations listed above?

5.5 Acting your way out: Disagreeing and apologising—with respect

A famous film star (I think Michael Caine) suffered from stage-fright. He cured himself by consciously acting the part of a character who felt perfectly confident.

Much of our life is spent acting different parts. You behave one way at home, another way in class, a third way with friends, because you are reacting to different people and different situations.

If you think about it, you realise that you could consciously change the way you behave in any situation you wanted. Sometimes you need to control the feelings you have, and you can do this by acting out different feelings.

Being assertive, not aggressive

Imagine you're making something, or doing some task. You might be cooking something, or mending your bike, or fixing your clothes, or clearing a table in your part-time job in a café. Another person looks at what you're doing and tells you it should be done a different way. You think your way is best. Write down what you're doing, and who it is who tells you to do it differently. Your answer will depend on who you're talking to, won't it?

Each person should find a phrase which can be used instead of something angry like, 'I don't care what you or anyone else thinks. I know what I'm doing. So get out of my way' or 'Mind your own business' or 'Keep your nose out of this.'

Here are some examples:

- 'I'm sorry, but I'm doing it the way I want.'
- 'You'll see in a minute that I'm right. This is how I'm doing it.'
- 'Thanks very much for your help. But it'll be better if I do it this way.'
- 'You've been a great help, but I'd like to try this out first.'
- 'You've certainly given me another idea, and I might change this bit. This is how I thought I'd change it.'

Take it in turns to make your statement as if you meant it, but politely, and with finality. If any statements come out hesitantly, the group should go round again. Try a firm gesture with your statement.

Disagreeing

Working in pairs, take one of the statements in the previous activity and invent two characters and a situation. Create at least two speeches for each character, including the statement you've chosen. Your situation might be social or political, with family, or friends, at school or work.

Accepting blame

Here are some of the things people say when they accept that they're wrong. Sometimes, of course, you say you're wrong even when you're not, in order to avoid an argument. You can probably think of situations like that. But at the same time, you need to preserve your self-respect.

You don't have to be crushed: 'I'm terribly sorry. I was wrong. Oh, dear. I'm hopeless. I never get anything right.'

There are better ways of accepting you were wrong:
- 'I see what you mean. I'll try not to do that again.'
- 'It wasn't totally clear. I'll make the correction.'
- 'Thanks for pointing that out. I see now how it should be.'
- 'I'll stop doing that. I can see how irritating that must be.'
- 'I'm sorry, officer. I had no idea I was doing that. I certainly am aware of it now.'
- 'Thanks, mate. I'll fix it. I can understand you being angry.'
- 'It was my fault. I do realise now. I'll make sure it doesn't happen again.'
- 'Yes, I understand. I'll try it your way and see if I can make it work.'
- 'Yes, I see. It's worth a try.'

Try these in turns, politely but not too humbly. You don't need to grovel.

Then in pairs, work out situations in shops, with the police, at work or school, or with friends where each one of these might apply.

Discussion

Can you think of any situation where you need to take a stand against assertive people? Think of a disagreement over the rules of a game, doing the housework in a shared house, keeping a dog from barking at night, how to run a social event.

When would you need to back down with dignity?

Even if you feel hurt and aggressive, or hurt and nervous, you can learn to control your feelings and speak firmly. You are more likely to get what you want that way than by acting angry and abusive, or apologetic and timid.

Notice how other people handle such situations. Of course, what you do needs to fit in with your personality. But you can change if you want to.

5.6 Who am I? All the men and women merely players

Do you behave differently with different people? Of course you do. Most people don't act the same with their grandparents as they do with their friends at school.

We've already looked at the idea that a person behaves differently in different situations. So in some ways we are all actors playing several different parts.

You have an idea of yourself as one kind of person. Your friends see you as another, and your parents as another again.

There are times when you have to pretend to be interested when you're bored, happy when you're sad, enjoying yourself when you're not.

A great time

In groups of three or four, work out a number of situations where you have had to pretend to be feeling something you weren't. Write down what the situations were. List as many as possible. For instance:

- 'It was a lovely party.'
- 'Just what I wanted!'
- 'Don't do that. Mummy's very cross.'
- 'That dress looks terrific.'

Discussion
What happens in these situations?

Why do people find themselves having to pretend to feel what they don't?

Why do you sometimes have to disguise your real feelings?

Would it be better if we were all honest about what we feel all the time?

Tactfully

In groups of three or four, choose one of the situations discussed below, and work out a conversation which illustrates how everyone behaves. Include parts for all the people in your group.

You can use these situations, or think of your own:

- The boss tells about his holiday at an office party. Everyone is bored but has to pretend to be interested.
- An old woman's dog has died. The dog kept the next-door family awake with its barking and bit the postman, but they realise she is upset and lonely.
- A cousin is giving a very dull (or wild) party. You and some others like parties which are noisier (or more under control). Out of consideration for your cousin, you try to enjoy yourself.

Don't you just love my new clothes?

- Your friend has invited you to the pictures with some other people. It isn't a film you like, but you want to please your friend.
- Your aunt asks you to lunch. Friends of hers are there. You try to join in politely with their conversation about their work and homes.
- One of your family has spent all their money on some terrible clothes. Then they ask the rest of the family for an opinion.

Variation
Now switch the situation, and role-play what would happen if you said what you really felt.

Variation
If you write the first as a play, put in brackets after each speech what the speaker really feels. For example:

JOHN: Yes, the colour suits you. (*You shouldn't wear lime green.*)

JEANETTE: Yeah, it's great. Can I borrow it sometime? (*I wouldn't be seen dead in it.*)
SHARON: You really think it's okay? (*I'm not sure, but if they think I look nice, I'll keep it.*)

Discussion

If you behave differently with your family, with close fiends, in class or tutorials, at work, out shopping, or at a party, which person is the real you?

Or does everyone have several sides to their personality?

Could you be that person in the other situations if you acted the part? For instance, could you be a home person or a cheerful school person when you're at an interview?

If not, what stops you?

Is it politeness, kindness, or lack of confidence?

Are most people happy with the kind of person they think they are?

Decide now that you're going to be the kind of person you want to be. You can still adapt to the best way to behave in different situations. Be patient. This takes time and determination.

5.7 Endings with a question: Don't you? Isn't it? Don't you think? Shall we? Will you?

We often end sentences with these words for opposite reasons:
  • because we're unsure if our listener agrees (polite, tentative, pleading)
  • to emphasise a demand (bossy, authoritarian, emphatic).
Are these added to be polite, or to demand something?
• 'But you want to come, *don't you?*'
• 'Leave those alone, *will you?*'
• 'It's quite pretty, *don't you think?*'
• 'Let's go to the beach, *shall we?*'
• 'It's okay if I borrow the car, *isn't it?*'
• 'I think we should go to Surfers, *don't you?*'

It depends on the situation (or the context), doesn't it? It also depends on how it's said, and on what word is emphasised.

Read the sentences aloud in a conversational voice. Note that the meaning changes, depending on the context.

For instance, look at 'Don't you' in the first sentence above. The emphasis is on 'don't', and then there's a hint of irritation. In the last sentence above, the emphasis is on 'you' and it's more like a plea or a request.

Tag questions

During the next two days, collect and write out at least three sentences you hear other people use, which end with one of these tag questions.

You might note down how tags are used in other languages. Some use 'no' or 'yes' as a tag at the end of a sentence, or 'please' as in German '*bitte*'.

We also use sounds like 'eh', 'huh', as in 'You didn't like the film, huh?' or 'You coming, eh?' Add these to your list.

Compare lists in class, and say what you can about the meaning the tags have.

5.8 Misunderstandings and exclusions: Dealing with others

They're laughing at me

We all make quick judgements about things that we see.

Have you ever thought someone was having a go at you, and then found that they were talking about something quite different? Or that they didn't even notice you were there?

You have to interpret events. But, like a good detective, you need to make a quick check of the evidence, before you jump to conclusions.

For instance, suppose a boy comes into the room and three girls laugh together. One boy, Harry, thinks, 'They're laughing at me. They think I'm stupid.'

Another boy, George, thinks, 'They're laughing to attract my attention. They like me.'

When the same happens to Dane, he simply goes over to them and says, 'What's the joke? Let me in on it.' The girls say, 'Just Sharon telling us about a dress she tried to make. It wouldn't interest you.' Dane feels rebuffed and wishes he hadn't approached them.

But when the same thing happens to Bill, he laughs, and says, 'Trust Sharon,' slaps her on the back and wanders off to find his friends, unworried.

Discussion

Harry, George, Dane and Bill interpret the girls' laughter differently.

Why? What determines how these boys behave?

Even when the girls say, 'It wouldn't interest you', the message the boy gets would depend very much on the tone of voice. They might be implying 'Mind your own business' or they might be apologising for not having a wittier joke to pass on. Or it might mean simply what it said, that it was something that interested the girls but wouldn't interest the boys.

Interviewed, and sacked

activity

Work in pairs. You're at a job interview. One plays the employer and the other the applicant. The employer comes round the front of his desk, shakes hands and pulls up a chair. The applicant mistakes this for easy-going equality, and treats the office like their own place. But the employer doesn't expect someone at an interview to be matey. Role-play how this misunderstanding works out.

In the same pairs, this time the employer calls an employee into the office, and begins, 'You've done a really good job.' The employee expects a promotion. But in fact the employer has to lay off six staff, including this employee. How do they both deal with this misunderstanding?

Invitation

Work in pairs. Chris rings Alex with an invitation. Alex doesn't want to go out with Chris, but also doesn't want to hurt Chris's feelings. Chris misunderstands and suggests solutions to each of Alex's excuses (washing hair, homework, visiting relatives, no money, has to look after the cat, etc.). How can this misunderstanding be sorted out?

Note that Chris and Alex can be boys' or girls' names, so you decide which they'll be.

Discussion

Why aren't we direct in our relationships with each other?

In kindergarten, a child says, 'Will you be my best friend?' and the other one says directly, 'No' or 'Yes.' Why doesn't this work when we grow older?

In the workplace, employers behave in one way to employees and in another way to other employers; similarly, employees behave in a different way to employers. Why? What would happen if there were no hierarchies? Would businesses still be able to function?

Do we have to have someone in charge, at home, at school and at work?

What would happen if we all said what we thought?

Should we always respect another person's feelings, no matter who they are?

6 Joining in

6.1 Role-plays for conversation: Park benches, tickets and romances

Do you sometimes find you're stuck for conversation?

Do you think small talk is a waste of time?

It isn't, because it's the way we get to know other people, and it's how we greet each other every day: 'Hi, how you going?' 'Isn't it hot!' 'How are you?' 'Did you see the game on Saturday?'

Do you ever find you can begin a conversation, but you have trouble keeping it going? For some people it's easy. Some even talk too much! For others, it's quite hard.

Try playing the role of a different person. That can help your conversational skills. You can say and do things in real life situations that you don't usually say and do.

Do you like to keep your distance? Or are you a back-slapper, a hugger, an arm-over-the-shoulder person?

Some people like to be close, and some don't. It can be a question of personal preference. But sometimes it's a cultural difference. Some cultures kiss in public. Have you seen French politicians on TV kissing visitors on both cheeks? Some nationalities shake hands; some keep a formal distance and bow instead. Most cultures have different rules for males and females, even if these rules are unwritten.

Have you ever squeezed into an overcrowded lift? People face the front and watch the floor numbers on the screen over the door. Of course they need to know when to get out. But it's also so that they don't have to look at the person squashed too close to them.

I need space

These exercises are also in closeness. In some of the role-plays, you have to be closer than one normally likes to be in a conversation.

You need plenty of space. You all have to talk, so don't do these plays in a room where you'll disturb others.

activity

Park bench

Work in groups of three, four or five. Set up four chairs in a row to look like a park bench. Decide on a character you'll play and write the name of your role on a sheet of paper pinned to your front. Some ideas are: clerk with sandwich, secretary, very large man, mother and child with ice cream, a drunk, solicitor in smart suit, chatty pensioner wanting to talk, weight lifter, punk.

First person comes along and decides to put their feet up on the bench.

Next person enters, squeezes in on the end while making a comment. (What would they say? Keep it in character: is it polite, rude, matter-of-fact?)

Third person simply shoves in, making another comment.

Fourth person stands facing the bench and requests permission to sit down. Two people make a space.

Once everyone is sitting down, they make remarks and conversation in keeping with their characters. You can speak to one character, or everyone in general.

Anyone can leave and return as another character. Don't forget to change your label.

How will you bring the play to an end? Perhaps the lunch hour ends: someone looks at their watch, and says it's two o'clock. Or perhaps two council workers come along and say they have to move the bench. Use your imagination.

You could practise this a few times. You won't have to do it for an audience. You just need to get it right for yourselves.

activity

Commuters

Work in groups of about six. The important thing here is to keep conversations going. It doesn't matter what you say, or if you interrupt someone else.

Decide on the parts each person will play. Two know each other, but the others are strangers. Decide on the relationship between the two. Are they business friends, or husband and wife, or two school students?

Stand in a row on the edge of the platform, waiting for a train. An express train rushes through. Everyone watches it from right to left.

Then the local train comes in. You wait for the people who are getting off, and then you all get on. It's full, so you are all strap-hanging, holding door-frames.

The two who know each other begin a conversation. The others join in with comments. The two ignore them and go on talking.

They might talk about plans to go to Surfers Paradise. Others could offer advice such as, 'I wouldn't go there. I got my wallet stolen' or 'Why don't you go to Fiji? It's pretty cheap' or 'My auntie went to Surfers. She had a great time.' Or they might talk about trouble with a girl or boyfriend, or someone in the office; the other passengers offer advice.

There's a jolt and they all fall on each other.

The train stops and some push out, excusing themselves with something like, 'Sorry. Excuse me. Got to get out here.'

The two finish their conversation. The others make passing comments to no-one in particular. The train stops and everyone pushes out.

activity

Queuing for tickets

Work in groups of about six. Everyone is queuing outside a ticket office. Decide whether the tickets are for a cinema, a train, a show, a sports event or a concert. You can talk about waiting and queuing, or about the event, or about anything you like. To make sure that everyone speaks at least once, the people in the queue should speak one after the other.

One by one, the people at the head of the queue go in and come out, and the people who are still in the queue ask them questions.

Then someone comes out and says, 'I've got the last one.'

The whole queue complains.

You can also do this without ever saying what you're queuing for. Keep your audience guessing.

A romantic play

activity

This is best in groups of three or four because you have to do some writing. Make up a play in verse. You can do a send-up or write a serious romance, whichever you like. Romances are usually very sexist with stereotyped submissive feminine characters and tough masculine characters. You can use these characters, or you can reverse them if you like. Or you can make the characters equal.

The *Dolly* poems were in rhyming couplets with four beats to a line:

> You said you'd always love me true,
> And I said I would love you, too.
> But now I love another one,
> So please don't try and spoil the fun.

Some rhymed in every second line, and had three beats to a line:

> You said you'd always love me,
> And I believed you did.
> When you found another,
> My desperate tears I hid.

Now *Dolly* poems are often in free verse. That means they have no rhymes and an irregular metre. Use this form if you find it easier. Here is an example of free verse spoken by two people.

SHE [*talking to another friend*]: I like to be alone, independent and free.

HE [*talking to another friend*]: I don't need anyone else.

SHE: But I was only pretending.

HE: It's just I hadn't met the right person.

SHE: Now I've found him and he doesn't notice me.

HE: What can I do? She has so many friends.

SHE: Give me some advice! Shall I dye my hair purple?

HE: Should I do something brave to make her notice?

In *Dolly* verse, try writing a very short romantic play. Each person's speech can be one line if you want, or a verse, or several lines. Does the boy find another girlfriend and the first girl get her revenge? Or does the girl find another boyfriend but the first boy wins her back somehow, for instance by a brave or kind act? Add other parts if you need them. Every person in the group should have a part.

6.2 Breaking in: Joining a conversation

Have you ever walked into a room and seen everyone talking in groups, and wondered which one to join?

When a person wants to break in to a group, how do they do it?

You might do any of these:

- listen to what the group is talking about and then ask a question

- listen and then add an anecdote about something which fits in
- burst in with a cheerful interruption, perhaps grabbing someone's arm
- push in between the two to force inclusion
- stand quite close and wait to be noticed and included
- find a person on their own and start a conversation with them.

Which group should I join?

Joining

activity

Working in threes, try the following. Two of you start up a conversation with each other. The third person wants to join in. You can try this either sitting down or standing. Change around so that all of you have a turn at trying to join the other two.

What did the third person do to try to be included?

What did the pair do? Did they welcome the third person, or try to prevent an interruption?

What are the most successful ways of joining in?

How much does it depend on the kind of person you are, and who the others are?

Keeping out

activity

Try the exercise again. This time two of you are so interested in what you're saying that you ignore the third person. Then change suddenly and welcome the third person. Change over, so that each takes a turn at trying to join in.

How did you feel when you were welcomed in?

How did you feel about keeping the third person out?

Human beings are social animals. We like to live in groups. In prehistoric times groups offered protection and help that was needed for survival. We like to join in, but they need to be people we feel happy with. You don't know whether you're going to like someone until you get to know them. So it's a pity not to try.

Groups give signals that they will or won't accept a new person. Sometimes a group is so involved in their conversation that they really don't notice someone trying to join in. Other times, they've formed such a close unit that they don't want to let anyone else in.

Usually, if you don't get a welcome fairly soon, you simply move off and find other people to talk to.

But some people are determined to join particular groups and will do anything to be let in. Small children sometimes try to bribe their way in with sweets—and usually lose the sweets and are left behind while the others run away.

In a new job, neighbourhood, or college, people usually play it fairly low-key for some time. They're simply pleasant to everyone, until they find out who they will fit in with. Often this takes quite a while, especially in a new job where the others have been working together for a long time.

In one small country town, a family were called newcomers for over twenty years because nearly everyone else had been born in the area. In jobs, the standard time for being accepted is about three months. People are normally advised not to throw their weight about before then. But they still have to make efforts to join in, and accept invitations to take part.

Discussion

How long does it take to fit in to a new place?

What does it depend on? For instance, in the first year at high school or university, everyone is new to the place, so they're all looking for groups.

What advice would you give to someone coming new to a place?

What advice would you give to someone trying to join a conversation?

Some people don't want to be in groups all the time. They like to be on their own to follow their interests, to unwind, and to have some peace.

6.3 Dealing with misunderstandings: Difficult situations

Have you ever had problems because you didn't understand what someone meant?

Do you sometimes say things that other people take the wrong way?

Although we can talk to each other, we are often misunderstood. We have to make a lot of guesses. And we jump to conclusions.

Saying what you mean

Work in groups of three or four. Imagine this situation in an office or shop.

Darren is new to the job, and has to ask Sue questions about the work. She's been working there for several months.

One day he waits for her at lunchtime, and follows her into the lift. He asks her where she's going to eat lunch. She says she's getting her hair done and goes off. The next day, Gordon tells Darren that he'll be in trouble for sexual harassment. Darren asks if Sue has complained about him. Gordon says, 'She said something to Toula, and Toula told me. I thought I'd warn you.'

There are several possible explanations for everything that's happened. Give as many reasons as you can for what each person says and does. Check on the evidence. Be careful not to jump to conclusions.

Why would Darren ask Sue where she ate lunch?

Why would Sue say she's having her hair done, without saying where she has lunch?

What could Gordon's reasons be for warning Darren about talking to Sue?

Why would Sue 'say something' to Toula, and what did she say? (What evidence does Darren have that Sue said anything? And how can he know what she said?)

Why would Toula tell Gordon, and what did she tell him? (How does Darren know she told Gordon anything at all? Or what she said?)

Now decide what you'd ask Darren, Sue, Toula and Gordon, so that everything's clear and there are no misunderstandings. What advice would you give to Darren?

Often problems arise in communication because we don't know what others mean by what they say and do. People misunderstand each other because they don't say clearly what they want.

And yet simply announcing what you want often makes things worse. You need to be tactful and persuasive. You have to choose the right time and place. You need to use the right words. Your tone of voice makes a difference, and so does the expression on your face. Even your position, sitting or standing, can make a difference. Often you need to plan ahead when you want to ask something important.

Getting it clear

In pairs or small groups, work out how you could deal most successfully and least successfully with the following:

- You are Darren and want to ask Sue out.
- You are Sue, and want to know if Darren is asking you out or just making polite conversation.
- You want to ask the supervisor to move you away from the person you are working next to, because you don't get on.
- Your neighbour has planted a tree which will block all the sun from your garden and you want it moved.
- You want to return something to a shop which doesn't work properly, e.g. a bicycle, a Walkman, power drill, a food mixer.
- You want to tell your girlfriend or boyfriend that you've decided to end the relationship.
- You want to tell a family down the street that their child scratched your car.

Discussion

There are no right answers to the following questions, because how you speak and behave might have many different results. It depends on the person you're speaking to, and how they behave.

In the problems above, was your aim to get what you wanted with the least unpleasantness and hurt to everyone? Or did you decide to express your own genuine feelings frankly?

What are some of the things that happen if people get angry and rude?

What are some of the things that happen if you answer rudeness politely, and anger calmly?

Can you be frank, honest and direct, and still be polite and protect the feelings of the other person?

Are there times when it's better to say that you're angry?

None of these problems is easy, because communication between two people is so complicated. You have to deal with feelings as well as facts. You must take into account not only your own feelings, but other people's as well. Sometimes you don't want to show your real feelings, but it's difficult to hide them. With all these complications, it's surprising that people manage to get on with each other as well as they do!

6.4 What a bore! Joining in conversations

You might have met two kinds of people who have no trouble talking, but others don't want to listen to them. One talks without a break and you can't get a word in. The other doesn't answer what you say, and talks on about their own interests, often on quite a different topic.

Holding forth

Work in pairs. Stand facing each other.

One person starts to talk about something that happened to them yesterday and keeps going as long as possible, while the other tries politely to interrupt.

When the second person succeeds in interrupting, they try to hold the floor.

No rude interruptions are allowed.

Know anyone with a motor mouth?

Ignoring the topic

Work in pairs again, standing facing each other.

One person begins by telling about something that happened to them at the weekend, and then leaves a pause for a response.

The other changes the subject totally, ignoring what the first speaker said.

The first speaker tries to go back to the first topic.

People use phrases like, 'As I was saying before …', 'There's just one more thing I wanted to say about …', 'To go back to what I was saying …' and 'If I could just say this …' to get back to the topic they want to talk about.

Keep up this conversation for as long as possible. Leave the other room to break in. Each one keeps to their own topic.

Discussion

Did you find that you wanted to include the other person in your conversation? Did you want to respond to what the other person said?

If you did, you're like most people. You usually want to make contact with the other person, to exchange ideas and stories. That's what communication means.

Most listeners want to respond to the one who's talking, so that the talk is two-way.

When you listen to speeches, you feel good if you're made to laugh, because this is an active response to the speaker. So is applause at the end of a speech.

When you speak to a group, most people will listen if you give them a chance. But they need a turn, too. If you don't get a turn to talk, you'll find it hard to keep listening.

6.5 Ways of being heard: Openings and conversational gambits

If you simply drop statements into a conversation, you take your listeners by surprise. Here are some openings that soften listeners up. If you don't use phrases like these, you don't always get listened to.

'The polished conversationalist is a familiar figure. He [or she] breaks smoothly into conversations, picks up the thread effortlessly, holds his listeners enthralled as he develops his point, and then elegantly bows out. How does he do it?'[1]

When people talk to each other, socially or at meetings, they don't simply state the bare facts of what they want to say. They use all sorts of openings to give a signal to other people that they expect to be heard. In that way, they prepare others to listen.

Here are some which you can try out.[2]

Fixing on a main point
- 'I have a question on that', 'Let's take up that question', 'One answer to that would be ...'.

Moving to another point
- 'This reminds me ...', 'Speaking of ...', 'Before I forget ...'.

Returning to a topic
- 'In any case ...', 'To get back to ...', 'Going back to ...'.

Fixing on particular points
- Several points: 'First', 'To begin with', 'First of all'; 'Second', 'Another thing', 'Next'; 'And finally', 'As the last thing'.
- A main point: 'The main thing is', 'Most of all', 'The real problem is'.
- An unusual point: 'Believe it or not', 'Strangely enough', 'You may not believe this but'.
- A difficult point: 'To be realistic', 'Let's face it', 'The catch is'.
- Emphasise a point: 'The main thing is', 'The most important thing is'.

Giving an opinion
- Guess: 'My guess is ...'.
- Opinion: 'I'm pretty sure that', 'I have reason to believe'.
- Belief: 'I honestly feel', 'I'm sure', 'Without doubt'.
- Personal view: 'I personally feel', 'I believe', 'The way I look at it'.
- Personal judgement: 'As far as I can tell', 'As I see it', 'It appears to me', 'To the best of my knowledge'.
- Personal experience: 'In my case', 'What I'm concerned about', 'For my own part'.
- Confidential: 'Just between you and me', 'Rumour has it', 'I hear on the grapevine'.

Suggesting action
- 'Why don't you', 'Here's what we can do', 'What I have in mind is'.

Adding to the topic
- Adding to a point: 'When it comes to ...', 'As far as that goes', 'In a case like this'.
- Adding an item: 'And another thing', 'What's more', 'I might add', 'Furthermore'.
- Giving a reason: 'The reason why', 'Seeing as how', 'On account of this', 'For this reason', 'Because of this'.
- Explaining a result: 'As a result', 'Consequently'.
- Possible outcome: 'In case of', 'If and when', 'As soon as', 'By the time'.
- Possible problems: 'Barring the possibility that', 'Unless'.
- Restating: 'What you're saying is', 'If I understand you', 'What I mean is', 'What I meant to say was'.
- Clarifying other's views: 'You may think ... but in fact', 'It may seem ... but actually', 'On the surface it appears as if ... but the truth of the matter is'.

1 Eric Keller, 'Gambits: Conversational Strategy Signals', *Conversational Routine*, F. Coulmas (ed.), Mouton, The Hague, 1981.
2 The list of phrases is in *ibid.*, pp. 93–113.

Making a judgement on the subject
- Doubt: 'Yes, but consider', 'Yes, but don't forget', 'That's fine, but', 'But the problem is'.
- Adding: 'Keeping in mind', 'Seeing that', 'Allowing for the fact that'.
- The other side: 'All the same', 'Yet on the other hand', 'Mind you, though', 'But then again'.

Arguing a point
- Generalisation: 'Most of the time', 'Again and again', 'Time and again', 'In general', 'Usually', 'As a rule', 'Once in a while', 'Every so often', 'Every now and then'.
- Exceptions: 'As an exception'.
- Examples: 'As an example', 'For one thing', 'To give you an idea'.
- Summarising: 'To sum up', 'In short', 'To make a long story short', 'In a nutshell'.

Taking turns in conversation
People who want to get into a conversation have other gambits.
- I want to have a turn: 'May I interrupt you for a moment?', 'Can you spare a minute?', 'I'd like to say something', 'I have something to say on that', 'Hey, have you heard this?'
- I want to keep talking: 'Wait a second [minute, tick, mo']', 'Well, let's see now', 'What I would say is …', 'I just want to add', 'Just let me finish', 'Just let me say this'.
- I've finished what I'm saying: 'That's about all I have to say on that', 'That's about it'.
- I don't want to join in: 'I have nothing to say on that', 'I'll pass on that', 'I really don't know'.
- You say something: 'So what do you think of that?', 'And what about you?' 'What have you got to say on that?'
- I want to leave the conversation: 'It's been nice talking to you', 'I'd better not take up any more of your time', 'I suppose I really ought to go', 'Well, I'll be seeing you'.

Listening, ready or not
Speakers give signals about whether they are ready to listen or be listened to. They also have ways of saying whether they accept what the other person has said. Notice that some of these are polite, others more abrupt; some are casual and others more formal.
- I'm listening: 'I'd like to hear about it', 'I'd like to know more about that', 'Go on' (different tone from 'Go on!' meaning 'You don't say!')
- I don't want to hear: 'I'm not really interested in that', 'I have no use for that', 'That doesn't concern me', 'That's got nothing to do with me', 'Why don't you leave me alone?'
- I want to give information: 'I've got something to tell you', 'Do you know what?', 'Well, here's what I think'.
- I don't want to give information: 'I don't know anything about that', 'I don't want to get into that', 'I don't think that really concerns you, does it?', 'That's none of your business'.
- I understand you: 'I agree', 'I knew that', 'No doubt about that', 'You said it', 'That's for sure', 'That's just what I was going to say', 'I know what you mean', 'That must be awful', 'I know how you feel', 'What a shame'.
- I don't understand or agree with you: 'I didn't know that', 'That's news to me', 'I don't think so at all', 'I can't agree with that', 'Serves you right', 'It's your own fault'.
- I don't quite agree with you: 'I don't think so, really', 'Do you really think that?', 'I

don't quite see that', 'Not that I disagree with you, but ...' (and other 'Not that ... but' statements).

- I want you to agree with me: 'Wouldn't it be a good idea ...?', 'What do you say to ...?', 'How about ...?'
- I agree with you after all: 'When you put it that way', 'Now that I think about it', 'On second thoughts'.
- I'll do what you want: 'I'd love to', 'I wouldn't mind', 'Why don't we, then'.
- I don't want to do what you want: 'I'm rather busy at the moment', 'I'd rather not', 'I don't think it would be a good idea', 'I'm sorry, I'm doing something else at that time', 'No way'.

Making sure the other is listening and understanding

There are other things we say when we want to make sure we're being understood or that we are understanding the other person.

- Are you understanding me? 'Are you following?', 'Do you see what I'm getting at?', 'Is that clear?', 'Right?', 'Okay?'
- I understood you: 'Okay', 'Sure', 'And so?', 'And then what happened?'
- I did not understand you: 'Excuse me?', 'Would you mind repeating that?', 'Sorry, I didn't get that last part', 'Could you say that again?', 'I don't quite get your point', 'What exactly do you mean?'
- You misunderstood me: 'That's not what I said', 'What I actually said is this', 'What I've been telling you all along is ...'

These gambits offer ways of breaking into a conversation, whether formal or informal; of staying in the conversation; of agreeing and disagreeing; and of withdrawing from the conversation. Most of them are used to keep the other person or people on side so that they'll continue to listen. Flat statements are often too abrupt, and don't save face. They often kill the conversation. These gambits help to keep communication open.

So practise these gambits until you find the ones that suit you best in the various situations you encounter.

7 Outside school

7.1 Going out: Conversation practice

You need to practise dealing with people in all sorts of other ways.

The best practice is *in vivo* (literally, *in life*), which means in the outside world, not in role-play.

Some of the activities in this book ask you to collect information outside, in interviews and so on.

Remember that your tone of voice says as much as your words.

You need to:

- practise polite openings and greetings: 'Good morning. I wonder if you have …'.
- practise getting attention: 'Excuse me, could you …', 'I'm sorry to interrupt, but would you mind …'.
- make the remarks which soften criticism: 'I'm afraid this is not …', 'I'm sorry, I didn't want …'.

On your own

Try out any of these:

- Make conversation with people who come to your home: visitors, friends of your parents, relatives, tradespeople and neighbours.
- Be polite in shops. Ask for exactly what you want. Show interest and concern. If you have to complain that what you've bought isn't right, do it politely.
- Ask in a library for information you need, or books on a subject that interests you. If you're polite, you'll be surprised how much help you are given.
- You might have to make phone-calls which aren't only gossip with friends. Enquire about jobs, or get any information you need. A good phone manner is a great asset in most jobs.
- Even in the bank, in the post office, or at the ticket counter, little bits of conversation make the exchange pleasanter and you get better service.

Working in small groups, report back, and tell each other your experiences.

7.2 Group passwords: Slang

Do you use the latest slang? Do you notice when other people, perhaps your grandparents, use slang that you've heard only in old films?

You learn how to fit into any new place by listening to what others say. Whether you're a child listening to grown-ups, or someone joining a new school or club, or an immigrant in a new country, or a worker on a job for the first time, you learn by copying others.

Different groups have different ways of talking. You don't have to be exactly like everybody else, but you do have to adapt. You want to find your own style. But you want to be part of a group, too.

Slang and group talk

Work in pairs or threes. Over about a week, collect as much up-to-date slang as you can. Make a different list for the slang that adults, such as your parents, use. List slang that your group thinks is just about out-of-date. And list slang that's the very newest.

What sort of words are they? There'll probably be lots of words which mean 'good' or 'bad'. (Books take a while to get into print, so anything I list here is bound to be out-of-date: groovy, ace, rad, super, grotty, daggy.)

Put together your lists for a dictionary of slang (below).

Don't include swear words or obscenities. These are offensive and inappropriate here. Knowing what's appropriate in different situations is one of the most important parts of this whole course.

Roving reporter

You'll need to do the first part of this outside the school. Work in pairs, or on your own. Go to any place where you can listen to people talking (e.g. at a take-away or fast-food place, a bench at a bus stop, in a shop, or on a bus, tram or train).

Listen to the remarks that people make to each other. What slang words do they use?

Afterwards (not in front of the people) make notes. (Many writers, reporters and researchers always carry notebooks, and make jottings when they hear something interesting.)

Compare your list with others. Keep it for the dictionary of slang.

Making a dictionary of slang

The class can put together a dictionary of slang. Give what the words mean; if you disagree on the meaning, give all meanings. The *Shorter Oxford Dictionary* gives sentences with the word in them, so that the meaning's quite clear. You could do this.

List whether the word is on the way in, in use, just out-of-date, or old-fashioned. Don't forget to date the dictionary, and to list inside the cover who wrote it and published it, with the address. That'll be very important if someone finds it in fifty years' time!

Formal Speaking

part three

8 Being heard by the audience

8.1 Thinking on your feet: Games for public speaking

How does your voice sound to you? It can be quite unnerving to hear your own voice when everyone else is listening. After you've played these games you'll be used to the way you sound. You need to speak loudly and clearly, so everyone can hear you. You can't get away with whispering!

Does your mind ever go blank when you're expected to speak to someone you don't know well, or when you have to answer a question? You can practise thinking quickly with these games. It's all a matter of habit, or 'mind over matter'.

Quick thinking, loud voice

You can work as a whole group, or the group can be divided into sub-groups to speed it up. Speed is important; this activity can become boring in a large group. You are practising quick thinking. What you say isn't important this time.

Round 1
You all stay seated, either in your normal places or in a circle. Each person in turn says a word, loud and clear. Try not to have any pauses. If you're stuck, you can say 'Pass.' The emphasis is on (a) speed and (b) using a loud, clear voice. You can whiz round the group again until everyone's voice is loud enough.

Round 2
Try the same again, but this time you mustn't say 'Pass.' If you're really stuck, you can repeat the word that the person before you said.

Round 3
You say a word, and the next person has to put the word into a sentence. The third person then says a new word, and the fourth one puts that word into a sentence. Thus every person has either a word or a sentence. Be ready for your turn, and keep up the pace.

Round 4

This time you start with a sentence instead of a word. For example, you might say, 'I went to a disco in the city.' The next person takes just one word from your sentence, for example 'city'. Then their sentence might be 'It's impossible to park in the city.' The next person might pick up 'park', and so on until everyone has had a turn.

You were sitting down for these activities. Now you need to really think on your feet. It's a bit more difficult to think quickly if everyone's looking at you and waiting for you to speak. It's harder still if you're the only one standing.

And yet it's very easy, really, to get into the habit of thinking quickly. You should be used to the activities by now, so here's a variation where you have to stand to speak.

On your feet

Try Rounds 3 and 4 again, with everyone seated. But this time each person stands when it's their turn to speak. Again, it's important to move quickly and to speak clearly.

8.2 No-one is looking at me! Public speaking exposed

Do you feel that everyone is staring at you when you make a mistake? Some people just think, 'Oh, well. Everyone's wrong sometimes.' But many people are afraid of public speaking because they feel as if they're stuck out there like someone facing a firing squad. If you're afraid that everyone is looking at you, try these activities. You'll find that it's even stranger if no-one is looking at you. How easy is it to listen when you're not looking at the speaker?

One word

Try this first in groups of five to eight, and then with the whole class. Sit in a circle. Close your eyes, and keep them shut all through.

The first person says any word, like 'dog', loudly and clearly. (Remember that this is practice for public speaking.)

When you've spoken, you touch the person next to you lightly on the arm or shoulder. Usually, you look at a person to show it's their turn, but this time, you can't because your eyes are shut. The next person must quickly say any word that reminds them of the last one, such as 'cat'. Go round the circle until everyone has had a turn. When the person who first spoke is touched by the last speaker, they say, 'This is the end.'

Repeat this until everyone can say their word without a long silence.

Open your eyes

Try it again with your eyes open. You don't need to touch the next speaker, because everyone can now see when it's their turn.

When everyone has spoken, move to the next activity, 'Story'. This time you have to talk for longer, but you can stop whenever you like.

Story

Work in the same groups. Again this activity takes place with eyes closed, but this time the first speaker begins a story and touches the next person when they run out of ideas.

You need only say a sentence, or you can go on for longer. If one speaker goes on for too long, the next person can touch their arm instead, to show that they want to speak.

Open your eïyes

Repeat this with your eyes open. Look at the next speaker when you want to stop, instead of touching them. You'll still need to touch the person if you want to interrupt them.

For the next activity, you have to listen carefully, as well as speaking.

Autobiography and listening

Again work in the same groups with eyes closed. This activity is best with groups of about six, so that people don't have to wait too long for a turn. The first speaker gives their name and something interesting about themselves, such as, 'I'm Sharon. I go hang-gliding and collect shells when we go to the beach on holiday.'

The second speaker must begin, 'Thanks, [*name*]. I was interested that…' and repeat very briefly what the last speaker said. For example: 'Thanks, Sharon. I was interested that you hang-glide and collect shells.' Then the second speaker gives their own name and something interesting about themselves.

Open your eyes

Now try this with your eyes open. Look at the whole group when you are telling about yourself. But look at the person you are thanking, when you speak to them. What you do with your eyes is very important.

When you're making a speech, you're usually standing while everyone else is sitting. Some people like this because it makes them feel in control of the group. But others feel very unsafe because they feel even more that everyone is looking at them. In these activities, of course, no-one is looking at you because their eyes are closed.

Stand up to speak

Try any of the activities above, still with eyes closed. But this time, you must stand up when you're touched on the shoulder or arm. You say your word, story or autobiography while standing, and then touch the next person on the shoulder before sitting down.

Open your eyes

Try these again, with everyone's eyes open.

Discussion

When your eyes were shut, did that make it easier or harder to speak?

When you couldn't see the speaker (because your eyes were shut), did that make it harder to listen?

Did you feel more comfortable because you knew no-one was looking at you when you spoke?

How did you react to being touched on the arm or shoulder while your eyes were closed?

Some people really enjoy having an audience. Once you get used to it, the response of an appreciative audience is very rewarding. Are you getting used to it?

8.3 Telling them: Describing and explaining

I'm trying to tell you about it!

....and is it meant to be sort of lumpy with green bits?

Sometimes you need to describe or explain something to someone else. How good are you at explaining? How much do they know already? What can you leave out? You might want to tell a friend the story of a film you saw, or how a video game works, or about a place you've been to. It's no good using technical terms to explain a computer program to someone who's never touched a computer.

In this section, you practise telling about a book or film, describing how something works, telling about a place shown in a picture, and describing a real place while you're there. Sometimes you'll need to prepare in advance. For other activities, you talk off the top of your head.

The story of a film or book

You can work in pairs, in small groups or as a whole class. Take it in turns to tell the story of a book you've just read, or a film you've seen.

If the whole class is studying a book or a film, take turns to tell about a chapter of the book, or a scene in the film. It's a useful way to get the story clear for everyone. Each person has a turn, but others can interrupt if they think the details are wrong.

Revision telling

If a novel is being studied in class, you can take a chapter each to prepare. It's a good idea to set a strict time limit, and to discuss beforehand what kind of detail the rest of the class will find useful. Is it the story-line, or the characters, or descriptions of the surroundings?

For instance, an outline of the story in one chapter could be given in 30 seconds. But if you want to comment on reasons why the characters did what they did, retelling the chapter will take much longer.

Each group of four could take one chapter, and each person in the group focuses on one aspect: the story-line, the characters, the place, the language.

At first, you might have a series of talks (30 seconds each) with everyone taking a turn.

Next, you could describe characters and so on, so each person has a different task.

You could try the same with your other subjects.

How something works

You can work as a whole class, with forums, or in groups of any size. You can use any subject for information: music, first aid, sport, cooking, carpentry, computer games, geography, literature, physics, chemistry, maths.

Your task is to explain to your partner or group how something works. You should speak for only a short time.

You should vary the sizes of groups during the lesson. For instance, a 50-minute class could spend 5 minutes working in pairs; followed by 10 minutes in small groups; then

15 minutes for a prepared forum of four students; ending with the whole group coming together to discuss the results for 5 minutes. About 15 minutes is needed for organising the groups each time.

If the whole class is the audience, you'll need to use illustrations such as lists and diagrams on the board, pictures or charts, an overhead projector or butchers' paper. Otherwise the audience finds it hard to pay attention. (Look at Chapter 13, 'Demonstrations'.)

If the material is for revision, you should check with the teacher that your material is accurate before presenting it to the class. You don't want them to learn the wrong things.

While you're talking, the audience needs to follow in their books, take notes and ask questions. This helps them to pay attention, and makes it easier for you to hold their attention.

You can use quite technical language when the audience knows the subject (as in a chemistry or woodwork class).

Is the material new to the audience? If you're describing chaos theory, or joisting techniques, or weather forecasting, to an English class, then you'll need to avoid technical terms. If, for instance, you're describing how scuba-diving equipment works, use simple language because many of the group won't know anything about it.

Tell a story about what happened to you. Personal stories make your explanations come alive, and hold everyone's interest. But don't make them too long.

Guided tour in a picture, or around the school

Have you ever been on a tour of a historic place and been led by a tour guide?

Here you're the tour guide and you're telling your group about a place they're looking at. Tour guides are usually well prepared, and relate interesting facts about the place and gossip about the people who've lived there.

Picture tour

Work in pairs. You each have a picture of a place (countryside, city, houses, inside a building or anything suitable you can find in magazines, tour brochures and so on; see below. You have a limited time (about 2 minutes) to show your visitor round. Talk as if you were both inside the picture. The tourist can ask questions. Use your imagination to make the tour as interesting as possible. Make up historical facts, ghosts, murders, or whatever you like.

Historical convict ruins at Port Arthur, Tasmania

Castle in England

Local tour

You need to go outside for this guided tour of the school. Groups of three will probably work best. Each group takes the class on a guided tour of a particular area (for instance, one group might do the classroom, the hall and corridor, and another group the library, the rubbish bin area and the car park). Remember that tour groups follow quietly along and listen carefully.

You might prepare ahead for your section, or this can be a spontaneous exercise where the leader picks on people at the time. Remember that interesting tour guides use:

- anecdotes about what someone did at a particular place: e.g. 'This is where …'
- a historical comment: e.g. 'This was the first part of the school to be built in 1956.'
- personal opinion: e.g. 'Personally I think something should be done about this rubbish area.'

You can use your imagination or stick to the true facts.

Your group could write a brief tour guide for your area, and all these could be put together to make a 'Guide to the School', which might be serious or might not.

8.4 Telling stories and jokes: Talking to amuse others

You spend a lot of time telling your friends stories about interesting things you've done. Or you might gossip about what other people are doing. These personal stories are sometimes called anecdotes. You spend more time in entertaining others this way than by telling set jokes.

Telling jokes is quite a skill.

There's the story of a man who went to a club, and the members were sitting round shouting out numbers. Whenever someone shouted a number, everyone laughed.

'What's all this?' the visitor asked.

His friend explained: 'All the jokes have been told so often that we decided to just give them numbers. Joke No. 1 is about the horse in the bathroom. Joke No. 2 is about the chicken crossing the road. And so on. When you want to tell a joke, you just have to shout out the number. Why don't you try it?'

Jokes are a great way to amuse your friends.

But when the visitor shouted out a number, no-one laughed.
'What was wrong with that joke?' asked the visitor.
'Nothing wrong with the joke,' said his friend. 'It was the way you told it.'

The way you tell it

You can do this in pairs. It's a quick exercise, a way of developing different tones of voice, so you can tell stories interestingly. Try a nursery rhyme everyone knows.

> Mary had a little lamb
>   Its fleece was white as snow,
> And everywhere that Mary went,
>   The lamb was sure to go.
> It followed her to school one day,
>   Which was against the rule.
> It made the children laugh and play
>   To see a lamb at school.

Take turns to say two or more lines as if you were speaking in one of the following ways:

- giving a sermon
- a judge summing up
- a policeman giving evidence
- expressing regret
- excited
- bored
- resigned
- sad
- sentimental
- a mother scolding her child
- speaking to kindergarten children.

Anecdotes

You can do this activity in pairs. Take turns telling about something that happened to you recently—on holiday, on a bike ride, coming to school, in a film you saw, at home.

Keep talking, as fluently as you can. You're talking about something you know well, so it's easy to keep going.

Time each other, so that to begin with, you talk for only 30 seconds each. Have several turns each.

Try to make your voice interesting, and remember that giving facts, not vague generalisations, helps to keep listeners interested. Don't just say, 'It was sensational; it was amazing; it was unbelievable; it was awful.' None of those give the listener any idea what happened. Give the facts.

Pieces of a story

Sit in a circle of about six or eight, or work as a class. The aim is to work as a group to tell a story, with each person speaking in turn. The leader keeps time, and signals (a bell works best) when 30 seconds is up. You can talk for less than 30 seconds, but not more.

Start with a story that everyone already knows (like 'Goldilocks and the Three Bears', or a film you've all seen), so that no-one is held up by not knowing what to say. You should try to follow on quickly, and keep talking, even if you say only a sentence.

When you're telling a joke or anecdote, sometimes a friend will interrupt you and tell you it doesn't go like that. This can be helpful—or irritating! This time, if one speaker gets a part of the story wrong, the next speaker can retell it. But the aim here is to be confident about telling a story to a group, so any corrections need to be tactful and polite.

Some stories or anecdotes which could be shared by the group are:

- a film or television show that everyone has seen
- a story that the group has just read
- what happened on a group excursion
- what happened in another class, like cooking, science
- the novel or play the group has been studying.

Telling jokes

Work first in pairs, and then in groups. Telling jokes is a special skill, and people who do it well often practise in private. If everyone laughs, or says it's a good joke, or even groans, you feel good. If no-one responds, or someone says they've heard it before, or says you've got it wrong, you should think, 'Oh, well. Better luck next time.' But some people feel bad and decide not to try again. That's a pity because people like to hear jokes.

For this exercise, you need to find a joke (see below; the *Readers Digest* is also a good source). Practise it.

Working in pairs, read your joke aloud, and respond to your partner's joke when they read it.

Then make notes of your joke, and tell it to your partner. Get some feedback: how can you improve?

The next step is to tell your joke to your partner without any notes.

After you are more practised, you can tell the joke to a large group.

A motorcyclist picked up a passenger and lent him his great coat to keep warm advising him to put it on backwards to keep the wind off his chest.

After a while he realised he wasn't there and turned back to look for him. He came across a group of people standing around his passenger in the centre of the road. Rushing up to them he asked if he was okay.

"He was" came the reply, "until we turned his head around".

Caution

Different jokes are appropriate to different people and in different places. Knowing what jokes are suitable is part of the skill of communication. Make sure your joke is suitable for this exercise. Sexist and racist jokes are not acceptable here (mother-in-law jokes ceased to be funny years ago).

8.5 Story with actions: Listening and moving

How often do you really try to listen, but find your mind wandering so you don't hear a word? When experts listen to a conference paper, their minds wander about every two minutes. With students at a lecture, it's more often.

If the speaker uses charts or something else for you to watch, it's easier to pay attention. If the speaker uses gestures and has a lively voice, people find it easier to listen.

You listen even better, if you can join in by speaking and moving some of the time.

Kindergarten or politics?

The following activity may seem to be kindergarten level, but politicians, religious speakers and those organising propaganda use it. Even serious adults find it absorbing to do. You may feel stupid at first, but this is part of the point. One of your aims is to overcome the feeling that others will think you are ridiculous. They're doing it, too. In the end, those who don't take part are made to feel more ridiculous than those who do. This is why propagandists and politicians find it so effective.

The idea is for the listeners, as well as the speaker, to use gestures.

You'll find that, because you have to fit your movements to the story or poem, you listen much more effectively. This is good for poetry, which is often hard to listen to if you don't have a copy in front of you.

activity

Listening with actions

The whole group can work together for this. The leader, or one of the group who reads clearly and not too fast, chooses a story, part of a story, a poem, or even a news report from the daily paper. The reader sits at the front. While the story is read, every member of the group must act it out. The listeners stay in their seats and use only their arms.

Variation: Individual actions

Make up your own actions while listening. Stay sitting in your chairs and keep quiet, so that everyone can hear the story or poem. You can use expressions and arm gestures.

Variation: Group actions

Two people sit at the front of the group. One person reads something. The other person sits beside them, and does actions to fit the reading. Everyone has to imitate the actions. Here is an example.

'Soup' by Carl Sandburg	Action
I saw a famous man eating soup	soup-eating action
I say he was lifting a fat broth	lift up spoon
into his mouth with a spoon.	open mouth and swallow
His name was in the newspapers that day	arms holding paper
Spelled out in tall black headlines	one finger pointing
And thousands of people were talking	
about him.	finger and thumb indicating 'yak yak'
When I saw him	finger and thumb circled round eyes
He sat bending his head over a plate	head down, make circle for plate
Putting soup in his mouth with a spoon.	soup-eating action

Variation: Small group following actions

Divide into groups of three or four. Each group chooses a leader. One person, standing at the front, reads out the poem or story. But this time, the group leaders decide on the actions. You copy the actions of the leader of your group.

Variation: Small group reading and actions

In each small group, every person chooses a few verses of a poem or a paragraph from a story. When you're choosing, think about the actions that others could do. As each person reads, the other three perform some actions.

Variation: Listening and moving

Clear a space in the room. The reader is at the front, but this time must read much more loudly and slowly.

The group act out what is being read. They can move where they like, in silent mime. You can't make any noise, or you won't hear the story. Here is an example, but you can find other stories.

> There was a loud knock on the door. The man opened the door carefully. He looked out. But no-one was there. He crept to the window. He undid the catch, and flung the window open, and peered out. He jumped back in horror. The giant beast clambered over the sill. It came slowly towards him. He stared it in the eye without flinching. The beast stopped in its tracks. It shielded its eyes from his powerful gaze. Then it turned and fled, scrambling out the window in terror. The man calmly locked the window.

Listening and talking

You can do these activities as a whole group. This time, the listeners speak, too.

Repeating last two words

Work as a whole group. The reader reads out the poem 'Soup'. This time the reader pauses for a moment at the end of each line, raises one hand, and repeats the last two words.

This is a signal for the whole group to repeat the last two words loudly and clearly and with feeling. For example:

READER: I saw a famous man eating soup. [*Raises hand, repeats*] Eating soup.
GROUP [*together, loudly*]: Eating soup!

Telling the action

Work as a whole group. Choose a story which has lots of action. One person reads it aloud, pausing after each action.

The group says together only the words that describe an action. It doesn't matter if everyone says slightly different words. The important things here are
- to listen for the words
- to speak loudly and clearly.

Find your own pieces to read, but here's an example.

SPEAKER: The tall, thin man opened the bedroom door carefully. [*Pause*]
GROUP: Opened the door.
SPEAKER: Very softly, he crept to the window [*Pause*]
GROUP: Crept to the window.
SPEAKER: With a trembling hand, he undid the catch, [*Pause*]
GROUP: Undid the catch.

SPEAKER: And violently flung the window open. [*Pause*]
GROUP: Flung the window open.

Variation: Speaking and movement

The audience can repeat the whole line after the leader, and do an action at the same time. This is a bit easier, as long as the lines are fairly short.

This poem is by Wordsworth, but you can choose something more light-hearted if you feel this makes fun of a serious poem. All the same, you'll find that you do listen to Wordsworth this way. And you also visualise the scene.

READER: I wandered lonely as a cloud
GROUP [*wandering round room*]: I wandered lonely as a cloud
READER: That floats on high o'er dale and hill,
GROUP [*waving arms and gazing upwards*]: That floats on high o'er dale and hill,
READER: And all at once I saw a crowd
GROUP [*putting hand to eyes*]: And all at once I saw a crowd
READER: A host of golden daffodils,
GROUP [*holding arms wide*]: A host of golden daffodils,
READER: Beside the lake, beneath the trees,
GROUP [*circling arms for lake, and showing trees above*]: Beside the lake, beneath the trees,
READER: Fluttering and dancing in the breeze
GROUP [*fluttering and dancing*]: Fluttering and dancing in the breeze.

8.6 A mixed bag for confident group talking: Nine activities

These are for practice in working as a group, and thinking quickly and speaking clearly so the whole group can hear.

You don't need to prepare for most of the exercises, although you may need to look up some facts beforehand. Remember, think quickly and speak clearly.

Brainstorming or buzz groups in the workplace are often run something like this, so that everyone has to contribute their ideas. It doesn't matter whether you think your idea is a good one or not, because it might spark off a useful idea from someone else. Many people think this is one of the best ways to get new ideas.

You might want to do only the group activity. The general discussion and individual writing activities are for those who want to go further.

Reaching an agreement

activity

Work in pairs. Each pair thinks up two characters who disagree, and writes their names and their problem on a card. Here are some examples:

- Dane wants to go the pictures and Maria wants to stay home and watch TV.
- Mother wants her son to wear a hat to keep off the sun, and he doesn't.
- Dad wants to watch the football on TV and Sonia wants a serial.
- Wayne wants to drive and Susan says she's a safer driver.
- Con wants to go to the pictures and Theresa wants to go to a disco.

Put all the cards in a box. Each pair takes one card. Take a character each, and develop the conversation until the two have agreed what to do about their problem.

Discussion

How were some of the problems solved?

Make headings for the kinds of solutions people reached: for instance, one persuades the other; compromise; one dominates the other, etc.

Now make headings for the kinds of argument which led to a solution; for instance, rational discussion; anger; sarcasm; refusal to talk; joking; dismissing the importance; bribery.

An argument simply means putting reasons and coming to a conclusion. It doesn't have to be angry. Why do we get angry when others disagree with us?

Bird poem

You can do this with the whole class, or with smaller groups.
- Each person writes down, in the middle of a line, the name of a bird that they think is most like them (e.g. *sparrow, eagle;* a noun).
- Now write a word in front of the bird to describe it (e.g. *busy, savage;* an adjective).
- Now put a word after the bird which tells what it does (e.g. *pecks, swooped;* a verb, present or past tense).
- Now write a word at the end to say how it's done (e.g. *greedily, swiftly;* an adverb).

Everyone should have four words. For instance: busy sparrow pecks greedily; savage eagle swooped swiftly.

Now each person reads out their sentence in turn, slowly and clearly, to make one long 'Bird Poem'.

Variation

Everyone writes their line on a strip of paper. Pin all the strips on a display board, adding some pictures of birds you've drawn or cut from magazines. Put your name under your bird poem if you want to identify yourself.

Alternatively, each person continues their poem, with their original line somewhere in the poem.

Brainstorming an issue

Sit in a circle in large groups, or the whole class.
- The first person makes a statement or gives an opinion about some event or issue: e.g. 'We should not cut down so many trees.'
- The second person adds an opinion or a further statement on the same topic: e.g. 'But we need wood and land to grow food.'
- The third person continues if possible. But if they have no more ideas on that topic, they can make a new statement on a different topic.

You should listen to other people's ideas, because if you are stuck for something to say, you can say, 'I agree with —— that ...' and repeat an earlier comment.

General discussion and writing

At the end, the group chooses one of the topics for a general discussion.

You could also use this method for brainstorming ideas and information for an essay on an issue or for a project the class is working on.

Group story, group tour

Sitting in a circle of about five or six, work together to tell the story of a film you've all seen, or a book you've all read.

Alternatively, plan a tour of a place you all know, such as the school, or the local shopping centre or town, or somewhere you all went on a camp. Each one of you takes the group to the next place. For instance, 'We start at the railway station', 'We cross the high street and look at the post office', 'We go into McDonald's and eat a Big Mac', and so on.

Not very serious problems and advice

Work in small groups, large groups or the whole class.

You begin, 'My problem is' and add whatever you like, whether serious or humorous: e.g. 'I don't have time to do my homework.'

The second speaker answers, 'My advice is' and gives advice: e.g. 'Do it as soon as you get home.'

The third speaker adds, 'I think you should': e.g. 'Do it at lunchtime.'

The fourth speaker begins, 'If I were you, I would': e.g. 'Explain to the teacher.'

The next speaker raises a new problem: e.g. 'I can't play the bagpipes.'

General discussion

Choose some of the problems, and construct some solutions to be written up like an advice column in a magazine. You could display these on a bulletin board or put them in a class newspaper.

Learning new facts

Work in small groups, large groups or as a whole class.

Easy version
Each person gives a fact about any topic, such as:
- local sport: e.g. Bartontown won the League Premiership
- the school: e.g. There are 800 students
- a historical fact: e.g. Henry VIII had six wives
- family history: e.g. My grandmother was born in a tent in the Sahara Desert in 1930
- local history: e.g. The oldest house in this suburb is in Smith St, built in 1880.

Serious version
You could use this in any class where the group is learning new information (e.g. environmental science; facts about New Guinea). You each give a fact from the topic you're studying.

If you can't think of a new fact, you can repeat a fact that someone else gave earlier. So you need to listen to others carefully.

The group should agree to a rule for correcting wrong facts. Either raise your hand and say, 'I think that …' and give your version. Or wait until it's your turn to speak, and make the correction then. Or, after each fact, the leader could ask, 'Does everyone agree?'

This works better than a short answer test, because the information comes from the group. Everyone is listening, so they're all learning the new facts.

ABC and Number Rhyming Couplets

Sit in a circle of any number. Warm up with the ABC exercise. The first person gives a word beginning with *a*, the second person says a word beginning with *b* and so on until you reach the end of the alphabet.

TRAVELLERS NEED BETTER DEAL: CANADIAN EXPERT

Melbourne's public transport system needed to increase service frequency and improve its public image to be comparable to systems around the world, a leading Canadian transport official said yesterday.

The head of Toronto's Transport Commission. Mr Mike Collie, said Melbourne had the basis of a good system but, to attract more users, it needed to overcome a perception of public transport being suitable only for commuters without a choice.

Mr Collie, who arrives in Melbourne today to meet the Minister for Major Projects and Conservation and Environment. Mr Birrell, said the high level of customer service on Toronto's transit system meant it was able to compete with car travel.

In Toronto, public transport accounts for 22 per cent of all trips, three times higher than in Melbourne, a city of similar population, size and car ownership. Toronto has had a 20 per cent increase in public transport use per person since 1965, while Melbourne's use per person has fallen 50 per cent.

'Any city has to be careful it doesn't become a city of roadways where public transit becomes a marginalised activity for the captive socio-economic group that have no other choice. Once you start to do that you create a different atmosphere in a city,' Mr Collie said.

He said the use of automated ticketing machines, to be introduced in Melbourne from October, would be a positive move that reflected international trends. The $100 million automated ticketing system, which will accept credit cards at larger stations, would be more efficient and convenient than paying cash for every trip, he said.

Mr Collie said Melbourne had to increase its service frequency and integrate train, tram and bus timetables to prevent commuters waiting at connecting points. 'If you have fewer off-peak service levels and people have to wait 20 to 30 minutes for trains, then they will take public transport use out of their daily life-style.'

In Toronto, the average off-peak public transport frequency was three to five minutes, compared with a 15-minute to 40-minute wait for Melbourne commuters, he said.

He said Toronto had recently started big construction projects on its transit network, including a $2.75 billion extension of two subway lines and a $220 million tramline.

Mr Collie said most European and Asian cities, unlike Melbourne, had continued to develop their public transport systems through the recession because of their social and environmental benefits.

By DUGALD JELLIE

Travellers need better deal...

Now try Number Rhyming Couplets. The first person begins with 'one' of any noun they like ('one frog').

The second person has 'two' and has to rhyme ('two dogs').

The third person can go on with that rhyme ('three logs'). Or they can begin a new rhyme, but continue with the numbers ('three bears').

The fourth person must rhyme with that ('four chairs'). And so on round the circle.

News and views

All the members of the group have the same text, such as an article from a newspaper or a magazine, like the one above, or a paragraph from a book. Read it through. Each person must refer to one section, read it out and make a comment, beginning with one of the following phrases:

- 'I think this part means …'
- 'This reminds me of …'
- 'I don't know what this bit means …'
- 'I like the part where it says …'
- 'These words … are good because …'
- 'I agree where it says …'

To begin with, it might be useful to write down the statement, but with practice you shouldn't need to. The aim here is for everyone to read the article and make some comment. When you've all had a turn, you should know and understand the article.

Story action

You need a group that isn't too big for this, about four or five.

Choose a very short story, such as 'Goldilocks' (or Roald Dahl's version of it). Each person reads a sentence aloud, and then asks a question about it.

The group answers in chorus, and makes an action to fit their answer. The members of the group won't always say exactly the same thing, but that doesn't matter. The important thing is to speak clearly and think quickly.

Example

FIRST PERSON [*reads*]: Once there was a little girl with golden locks called Goldilocks. [*Asks the group*] What did she have?

CHORUS: Golden locks. [*Members of group touch their hair*]

SECOND PERSON [*reads*]: One day while out walking, she found a house in the forest and opened the front door. [*Asks the group*] What did she open?

CHORUS: She opened the front door. [*They make door-opening actions*]

Workplace groups often do activities like these, though they might seem rather simple for adults. They encourage groups of people to work together, and they encourage every member of the group to make a contribution. If you're in a job and being paid to work, you'll be expected to give your ideas—and to listen to other people's ideas. People who speak softly often don't get heard. And people who speak confidently often don't listen to others. Either way, good ideas are wasted.

9 Interviews

Ray Martin interviewing guest (Olivia Newton John)

Have you ever been interviewed? What was it for?

Can you name someone you've seen interviewed on television? Why were they being interviewed?

There are two reasons for interviewing someone:

- You might be applying for a job, or a place in a course, or to join a group of some kind. The employer, or a person in charge, interviews you to see if you're the right person. They'll know something about you already if you've written an application.
- Or you might be interviewed for television, or by a researcher, because you're an interesting person for some reason.

How many types of interview can you list? Can you give examples you've seen, especially on television, of the following?

- People are interviewed for newspaper articles or on television. The interview can be arranged ahead, or you might be stopped in the street or at your front door without warning.
- You might be interviewed over the phone by someone doing an opinion poll on the Prime Minister's popularity for the press, or market research on pet food.
- You might be picked by chance by a roving reporter.
- You might be hounded if you've done something famous or criminal or tragic.
- If you're well known, you might be respectfully interviewed and paid for it as well.
- Some people want to be interviewed, like politicians who want votes, writers who want to sell their books, or protesters who want publicity.
- Some people avoid interviews, especially if they have suffered a tragedy or been in a scandal.
- Interviewers may be formal and encouraging (for a job); or very polite and flattering (with a popular celebrity); or quite rude and challenging (with a politician); or pushy

and tactless (when chasing up unwilling people who've been in the news).

- The interviewer might seek to keep most of the attention (if the audience is more interested in the interviewer, as with television personalities). Or the interviewer might keep out of the picture (so you never see the interviewer, who interrupts as little as possible).

What makes a good interviewer? What makes a good interview subject (interviewee)?

Interviewing is a real art. A good interviewer gets people to say more than they mean to, because they feel comfortable and trusting.

Being interviewed is an art, too. Good interviewees come over looking and sounding their best, and don't get trapped into saying more than they intend to.

The importance of body language and voice

Both the interviewer and the person being interviewed give information to the other by their movements and their tone of voice.

If you're interviewing someone, you need to sound confident, enthusiastic, concerned, encouraging, and sometimes firm. You need to speak clearly so the other person can hear the question. Otherwise you won't get people to talk to you. And you need to keep control so the interview doesn't wander away from its topic or purpose.

If you're being interviewed, you need to consider your tone of voice. Your non-verbal communication or body language is important, too. How you sit, how you dress, how you move, all come into that. You need to be relaxed but not sloppy, keen but not humble, confident but not pushy, friendly but not matey.

9.1 Emphasis on the interviewer: Conducting an interview

It is unlikely that you will ever be interviewed in front of a live audience, so there's no point in practising in front of the whole class. Work in pairs, or in groups if several people are needed for the interview. Some pairs could perform in front of the class as models for others to see.

In opinion interviews and celebrity interviews, the person being interviewed can behave however they like, though celebrities want the viewers or readers to approve of them. You can be rude, or politely refuse, if you don't want to be interviewed in the street. You can be quite eccentric if you're a celebrity and people expect it—as with some sportspeople or pop stars. But the interviewer has to be polite and has to persuade the person being interviewed to tell what people want to hear. So the interviewer needs to be diplomatic and persuasive.

Street interview

Work in pairs. You have a roving microphone and collect opinions on a current local issue. List several issues. Take it in turns to be the interviewer.

Work out the questions first. Interviewers always plan questions ahead. Answer in as much detail as possible. Remember that this is an exercise in fluent talking, so try to help the interviewer.

Example

INTERVIEWER: Excuse me, do you have a moment? Could I ask you what you think about closing the swimming pool?

SHOPPER: If it's dangerous, then they should close it.

INTERVIEWER: The council says it's because the local kids are causing trouble there. What is your opinion on that?

SHOPPER: They've got to let off steam somewhere. They should get someone who can control the kids at the pool.

INTERVIEWER: You've got a point there. Thanks for your opinion.

Front door interview

Work in pairs (or threes, with two people answering the door). You could be getting answers to a questionnaire run by the local council. Or you could be a reporter trying to get more information about the family next door who've been in the news.

Example

WIFE [*answering door*]: Yes? What do you want?

INTERVIEWER: I'm from the local council. We're trying to find out what householders think should be done to improve this suburb.

WIFE: They should collect rubbish more often. Sweep the streets occasionally. Put up notices to stop people letting their dogs mess on the nature strip. That's illegal, you know.

INTERVIEWER: Yes, the fine is $250.

WIFE: People don't know that unless they're told. They ought to have notices up.

HUSBAND [*appearing*]: They should take the humps out of the street. Ruin your car. And put a pedestrian crossing by the milk bar. And cut out the dinners the council members give themselves. You can tell them that from me.

Telephone interview

You often get telephone calls at home from interviewers conducting opinion polls and doing market research. Newspaper polls are conducted nearly every week, asking what people think of politicians or unemployment or the economy. Some surveys are a list of fixed questions with one-word answers. In others, the interviewer has a fixed script beginning with something like, 'Hello, how are you this evening? We've chosen you … etc.' Others ask for ideas.

Businesses use the telephone to sell services. It's called 'telemarketing'. Charities often use the telephone to request donations.

There are also talkback shows on the radio, where the interviewee telephones the interviewer. Often an opinion is given by an expert and people ring in with their opinion or comments.

Example: Market research interview

INTERVIEWER: Hello, is that Mrs Stavros? I wonder if you have a moment to answer some questions about your favourite food.

MRS STAVROS: I like most things.

INTERVIEWER: What do you like to have when you go out to dinner?

MRS STAVROS: We don't usually go out.

INTERVIEWER: If I list some things, could you tell me whether you like them very much, a little, or not at all: hamburgers … fried chicken … hot curry … fish and chips … spaghetti Bolognese … pizza. [MRS STAVROS *answers each one of these*]

MRS STAVROS: Ah, now I'll tell you. The thing I like most is spaghetti marinara and this is how I make it …

The interviewer doesn't want recipes. How does he or she deal with that?

Complete this interview.

Now make up a telephone interview to carry out market research on another set of products, or an opinion poll on some social or political question. Newspapers and journals, like the *Australian* and the *Bulletin* take polls on questions such as how people spend their time, what sports facilities they use, how they feel about marriage, among others.

When you have written the interview questions, try them out on each other. Change pairs and try it with another interviewee.

Talkback show

In groups of five or six, arrange a talkback show. One of you reads out a statement or a question, such as how a local park should be used, whether heavy metal music is subversive, that marriage is an out-of-date convention, that dogs' beauty parlours are a sign of decadence, or that schools should have cafeterias as they do in the USA and England.

You need a host or compère—the person who runs the radio show. This person asks for callers, says hello to them, and stops them if they're talking too much, or are rude, or spoil the show. The rest of you are callers.

Example

HARRY, THE HOST: I want to introduce today Ms Germaine Sheppard, who has a very special business in High Street. Good morning, Germaine.

GERMAINE: Good morning, Harry, and good morning, listeners. I run a dogs' beauty parlour and I find many people will spend money on their dogs' coats that they won't spend going to the hairdresser. They love their dogs like babies and nothing is too good for them. We do shampoo, flea control, trimming of coats and of claws, styling for poodles and English sheep-dogs. We also provide a variety of scented flea powders—pine forest, rose, gardenia and musk. We sell bows for top-knots, diamanté collars, silk walking coats, the dogs' doona, and the newest thing from Japan, the dogs' futon. We really look after dogs.

HARRY: Thank you, Germaine. I wonder if our listeners have any queries about dog care. Germaine will answer your questions. First caller. Hello, Susan.

SUSAN: Hello, Harry. I love your program. I listen every day. I'm just doing the ironing. I think it's a wonderful …

HARRY: Thank you, Susan. Could we have your question?

SUSAN: I take my dog for a shampoo and set every week, and she looks just lovely. There's one worry. When I put her in the car to go there, she goes mad. I can hardly drag her in. Why's that?

GERMAINE: It wouldn't happen in my parlour. Susan. Dogs love coming here. Perhaps the switchboard can give you the address.

HARRY: Thank you, Germaine. And thank you for your views, Susan. Next caller. Hello, George.

GEORGE: I think it's the biggest load of rubbish I've heard in a long time. It's a waste of money. Even the dog hates it. She said so. It's cruelty to dumb animals and especially considering the state of the economy …

GERMAINE [*interrupts*]: You obviously aren't a dog-lover. Some people have no-one to love but their dogs.

GEORGE: You love it because you love the money. What do you charge, may I ask? I bet you …

HARRY: Thank you, George, for your views. Next caller. Hello, Jenny.

You could finish this one with two more callers, and then do your own talkback show. Everyone in the group must take a part.

Media interview

Work in pairs or threes. One is the interviewer and the other one or two are being interviewed. Sit in chairs facing each other. You're in a television studio and there are cameras, but no audience. The people being interviewed can play the parts of well-known sports or music celebrities, or be themselves.

Plan the questions in advance. Find out everything you can about the person to be interviewed. Interviewers for the media have to be sure beforehand that there won't be silences or embarrassing comments.

Watch some television interviews. Note how the interviewer opens the interview, what sort of questions are asked, how much the interviewer talks, and how the interview is brought to an end.

The interviewer should give both people being interviewed an equal chance to speak.

The people being interviewed should try to be as interesting or amusing as possible, because this is their best publicity. They want the audience to like them.

Example

INTERVIEWER: Welcome to the Channel 8 Celebrity program. Now, Carl Schmidt, you have just won the Australian Tennis Open, and you were only fifteenth on the list. Is this your first big win?

CARL: Yeah. I was really astonished. I didn't seem to be able to do anything wrong. I'd won a few local tournaments, just enough to get in to this one.

INTERVIEWER: And you, Charenne de Botte, you've had a great win, too, with the Women's Open. You won in France, didn't you?

CHARENNE: Yes, Daniel, I did. But the Australians are a wonderful crowd, and I wouldn't have won if they hadn't been behind me.

INTERVIEWER: What's been the most important thing in helping you get here? Who would like to go first?

CARL: I owe it all to my aunt. She had a tennis court … etc.

Continue the interview from here, with Carl telling his story and Charenne also taking a turn. You could end it like this.

INTERVIEWER [*ending*]: Thank you, Charenne and thank you, Carl, and good luck for the future. I think it's the Mexican Grand Slam, isn't it?

CARL and CHARENNE [*together*]: Yes, it is. Thank you.

9.2 Emphasis on the interviewee: Being interviewed

When you apply for a job or a course, you're likely to be interviewed. Especially in job interviews there's an accepted way of behaving which you need to know. Of course you don't have to follow these rules, but you mightn't get the job. You're sometimes advised to be 'natural and relaxed' but if being natural means you chew gum, use unsuitable language and put your feet up, obviously you aren't going to get far in some interviews.

The interviews we've looked at so far are hardest for the interviewer, who has the responsibility for keeping the interview going, getting the right information, and making it interesting. With the next lot of interviews, it is the person being interviewed who's under pressure.

Sometimes people are interviewed to be selected for particular courses when there is a quota, or when certain personal qualities are needed as well as ability.

Course interview

activity

Work in pairs. Decide on the course (it can be anything you choose, whether interviews are normal or not). Between you, make a list of the qualities you think are needed for such a course (reliability, calmness, kindness, toughness, outdoor experience, experience with children, confidence, etc.).

Find out as much as you can about this particular career. Research is important for the interviewer, of course, but the person being interviewed should have done some too.

When you have the information, the interviewer makes a list of questions. The interviewer decides whether the applicant needs to be put at ease or put on the spot— whatever will make them show what they are really like.

What kind of impression do you want to make? Should you be very confident, friendly, polite, modest, earnest? How much should you talk? Should you ask questions? What should you add that the interviewer hasn't asked?

Example

INTERVIEWER: Good morning. You're Tanya Sekados, is that right? Please sit down. You did well in the exam so you've been chosen for an interview. But we've only a few places in the course and we want to be sure we get people who really want to become a ——. Can you tell me why you would like this career?

TANYA: I had always wanted to be an engineer like my mother. But two years ago I did work experience as a —— and since then I've taken every opportunity to find out about it. I like doing —— and ——. I'm particularly good at ——, I think.

INTERVIEWER: How do you feel about doing ——? It isn't always pleasant and it can be very tiring …

[*And so on until the end*]

INTERVIEWER: Do you want to ask any questions?

SUSAN: There's always publicity about —— earning $100,000 a year, but I've read that the average is about $30,000. Is that true?

INTERVIEWER: Yes, only very few people earn the big salaries.

SUSAN: I think I'll feel lucky to earn $30,000. It's the type of work you do that matters most, and it's what I want to do.

INTERVIEWER: Well, I think that's all. Thank you, Tanya. We'll send out offers within the next week.

Job interview

Work in pairs. Find a number of jobs or apprenticeships advertised in the local paper or a national daily paper.

For each advertisement, find out what you can about the firm, the work done in that job, and what the usual requirements are. It's useful to ask a friend or one of the family about their firm and the work they do. Both the interviewer and the person being interviewed need to know all about the job.

The applicant has already sent in an application with qualifications, age, experience and so on. The interviewer plans some questions.

One of you plays the interviewer and the other the applicant. Then exchange roles and repeat the exercise. See if you are both better at it, having seen how the other one behaved.

Example

INTERVIEWER: Come in. It's Grant, isn't it? Please sit down. Now, you've said here that you have a forklift driver's licence. What work have you done with that?

APPLICANT: I've had it for six months. I move the sacks in the nursery and the heavy plant pots. They break easily. You've got to be careful. I haven't broken any. [*Smiles*]

INTERVIEWER: Work begins at 7.00 a.m., and tools have to be put away before you leave. How do you feel about that?

APPLICANT: I'm used to that. I don't think I've ever been late for work. One day a week, I was the one who had to lock up. My boss trusted me with that.

INTERVIEWER: In this job, you'd be in charge of two casual workers. You'd have to work out their jobs for the day and check that they were done. Have you ever been in charge of other people?

APPLICANT: Well, no, not actually. But I've been responsible for deciding what jobs I'd get done each day. I don't think I'd have a problem working it out for three people—myself and two others. You'd have to be a bit tactful checking up on them, wouldn't you? Do your own job properly, I mean. I think I can do that.

[*And so on*]

INTERVIEWER [*at the end*]: Well, thank you very much, Grant. We'll let you know in a few days. If you're trying for other jobs, hold off until you hear from us. Though I can't promise anything, and we've had a lot of good applicants, I think you've got a chance.

Panel interview

Work in groups of four. Some interviews are conducted by a panel of two or up to six people, depending on how important the job is.

Panel members ask questions that they think are useful. Sometimes they are more intent on impressing each other than on listening to the applicant. In some cases, each member is an expert on a particular area, and their questions focus on that.

Decide on a job. You can look in the *Australian*, or the local paper. Select one person to be interviewed and three as panel members. Give the panel members one of the following positions, or think of your own:

- the equal opportunity representative
- the union or professional association representative
- an expert in the job area
- the senior partner in the firm who is more or less retired and there out of courtesy.

Work out questions that each panel member would need to ask and what answers they'd be looking for.

When you're being interviewed by a panel, it's hard to decide which person to talk to, who to look at, who to agree with if two panel members disagree, how much to add to questions, and how long answers need to be. After all, four people are talking, not just two.

When you've completed the interview, change places until everyone has had a turn.

Discussion

What's the difference between interviewing someone, and having a conversation with someone you've met for the first time?

What are some of the most important things you've discovered about interviewing someone?

What's the hardest thing about being interviewed?

Do you think it would be easier if you were in a real interview?

Keeping a conversation going

Work in pairs. You will be called A and B.

First, A starts a conversation. B has to keep it going.

Then B starts a conversation. A has to be discouraging.

Discussion

What keeps a conversation going?

Where do you look when talking to the other person?

There are two purposes of interviewing: to judge someone or to find out about someone. How do they differ? In what ways are they the same?

What makes the person being interviewed nervous?

What is the interviewer trying to find out?

How does the interviewer want to make the person being interviewed feel?

This last question is an important one for both interviewers and interviewees to think about.

Interviewers sometimes seem to want to make the people they are interviewing feel uncomfortable, and sometimes they seem to want to put them at ease.

How do each of these work for the interviewer?

Some people in interviews are on the defensive straight away and appear hostile when they don't need to. Or sometimes they are so at ease that they say things they wish they hadn't.

9.3 Interviewing outside: Questions for information

Do you find it easier to ask someone for information, or to make conversation at a party? It depends on who you are.

Is it easier to talk to new people if you have a friend with you? Most people think it is, because they've got some support. But some people feel more confident if they don't have anyone else watching.

Have you done any projects where you have to interview people outside the school?

This time, you'll be doing some of your talking outside the classroom, and reporting back to the group.

Tape recorders
Sometimes people use an audiotape recorder for interviews, but it takes a long time to transcribe the tape. Notes are easier to deal with. If you do use a tape recorder, the best idea is to listen to the recording a few times, and take notes from that. It enables you to check up on points that you missed.

Solo outside interview

Work in groups of four. Each group selects one topic. Here are some ideas:
- What did children do for entertainment when your parents or your grandparents were children?
- What do people of different ages eat for breakfast?
- What are people's favourite cars and why?

- What would you do with a million dollars?
- What do you think of the government?

Each member of the group interviews someone outside the class, and reports on what that person thinks, or what they know, about this topic.

- Plan the questions, including polite ways of approaching the person. How will you begin?
- Practise your questions with each other beforehand. Have a firm backing or a clipboard to write on.
- Arrange to interview the person somewhere quiet. Introduce yourself.
- Put your material together in a report, writing it so that others will want to listen to it. Make it interesting. Include:
- your topic
- where you went (describe the place)
- who you asked (age, sex, attitude)
- what they said
- what you concluded about their views (typical, biased, unclear, precise).
- Practise reading your report aloud. Read your report clearly and slowly to your small group.

Presenting your results

Work in the same groups of four to make a presentation to the whole class. You should work together to combine your four reports into one. Practise so you can present it to the class without stumbling.

Limit the time to 5 minutes or so. The aim of this exercise is to have everyone take part in a presentation. The content is not the main purpose, as it might be in a subject lesson.

All four should sit at the front of the class to make the presentation. Everyone should take part in speaking.

Decide whether all four will speak equally, or one will be the main speaker and the other three will add small sections.

Example 1 (1 minute each)
- The first speaker begins by stating the topic.
- The second speaker says who you decided to interview and where.
- The third speaker summarises the answers you got in interviews.
- The fourth speaker concludes by saying what you found out about your topic.

Example 2
- First speaker describes the topic (2 minutes).
- Each person says briefly who they interviewed and what the result was (all four speakers, 1 minute each).
- First speaker gives a brief conclusion.

This activity could be part of another assignment in English or another subject. If interviews have been arranged in the local community, you might find it helpful to work in pairs.

9.4 Asking questions: A study topic

Have you ever wanted to ask a question, but didn't like to?

Or felt you should ask a question, and couldn't think of anything to say?

Or didn't want to admit you didn't know?

Asking questions should be easy, but sometimes it isn't.

Asking questions is as important as answering them. At work or at school, many people make mistakes because they didn't like to ask, or didn't know how to ask, or thought people would think they were stupid for not knowing already. It's better to ask dumb questions than to make dumb mistakes.

Have you ever known the answer, but not liked to say so?

Or tried to answer, but you didn't get asked?

Or given the right answer, but been misunderstood and told you were wrong?

Usually, in a class discussion, about six students do all the talking, about six keep quiet, and the rest say a few words.

If there are twenty-five students in a lesson lasting 50 minutes, how much talking could each do? Have you left out the teacher? Everyone expects the teacher to do most of the talking.

The purpose of these activities is to have everyone asking questions and everyone answering. The idea is to have your voice heard. The activities are not intended to test how much you know, or to make judgements about how good your question or answer is. They are for practice in being heard.

Questions about the text

Work in pairs. Each of you think of four questions about a text that the class is studying. You could ask your partner for an opinion: 'What do you think of the ending?' Or ask for facts: 'How does X character sort out his problems with Y character?'

Answer as clearly as possible. Did you know the answer to the question you were asking?

Sharing the answer

Work in groups of four. This time each person thinks of a question based on a story or film you're studying. You can plan these ahead.

Each one of you takes a turn at answering, without anyone else interrupting. If you don't know, you can say so, and someone else answers.

When you've run out of things to say, you should ask, 'Does anyone else know more about that?' In this way, you should all find out more about the answer. It's a good idea to try this after watching a video, as everyone will have something to say.

Questions in a box

This is for groups of six to eight, or the whole class. Each person writes down a question on some recent work the class is doing on a story or film, or any agreed subject.

Sit in a circle. Put the questions in a box. Pass the box round, and each take a question in turn.

Look at your question. You can reword it in any way you like. Turn to the person on your left, and ask them your version of the question you have.

They should answer briefly. If they don't know, they must add something helpful: for instance, 'I don't know, but you could look it up in the library' or 'I don't know, but it might be something to do with …'. Then move on to the next question.

This exercise is not a test of knowledge. The purposes of this exercise are to practise:
- rewording questions quickly
- answering in a positive and confident way.

Extension

Once everyone is used to answering with confidence, this is a good way to revise for tests. Then, of course, it becomes a test of knowledge—but you are all helping each other to learn.

If one person doesn't know, then the person who wrote the question should answer it. To speed up the exercise, the teacher could give the answer.

10 Speaking on your own

Speaking on your own to a group takes courage. People who don't feel nervous aren't always the best speakers. Some very famous speakers have been extremely shy and nervous, and have taught themselves to speak well in public.

There are various situations in which you might find you need to speak in public.

- You can chair a meeting, or a speech session where you introduce the speaker. Or you can be asked to welcome an official guest, or give a farewell present to someone. There are rules for all these.
- You can speak as part of a team, in panels, forums, and debates, where other team members support you.
- You can give a report, a talk or a speech, where the audience sits quietly to listen to you. There may be arrangements for them to ask you questions at the end.
- You can conduct a tutorial, a seminar or a demonstration, where you ask the audience to take part, to ask and answer questions.

You can do all of these. The secret is to prepare, and practise. You can't learn by just reading about public speaking. You can't learn by watching other people speak in public. You can only learn by doing it yourself.

Method

Read, observe, prepare, practise, read some more, watch others again, and then prepare and practise and practise and practise—and finally get up there in front of your audience.

Rules

Anyone can learn to speak to a group. Everyone feels apprehensive some of the time. That is reasonable, because the speaker needs to hold the attention of the audience, and audiences are sometimes not very good.

Speakers gain confidence by having some success. That is why, in these exercises, the rules are so important. Remember, these are learning exercises and the audience is part of the learning group.

There are rules or conventions for most types of public speaking. You'll find it easier if you know the conventions, because they actually help both you and the audience.

Rule 1

The speaker must prepare thoroughly, thinking of what will keep the audience listening. Nervous speakers are often poor speakers because they fail to prepare.

Rule 2

The audience must pay attention so that they can make helpful comments to the speaker afterwards. Audiences can help or hinder speakers.

Rule 3

The speaker need never be up in front of the audience alone. A person acting as Chair should sit beside the speaker to introduce, support and thank the speaker.

Rule 4

The audience must applaud whenever asked to do so by the Chair. This may be when the speaker is introduced, and it will be when the speaker has been thanked at the end. Applause builds confidence. There must be as much applause for nervous speakers as for confident speakers. In fact, the nervous speaker needs it more.

All the exercises in the following chapters require you to speak on your own to an audience, usually the whole group.

Arranging the room

The placement of seats and tables varies according to the type of public speaking that is to take place. This diagram shows some typical arrangements.

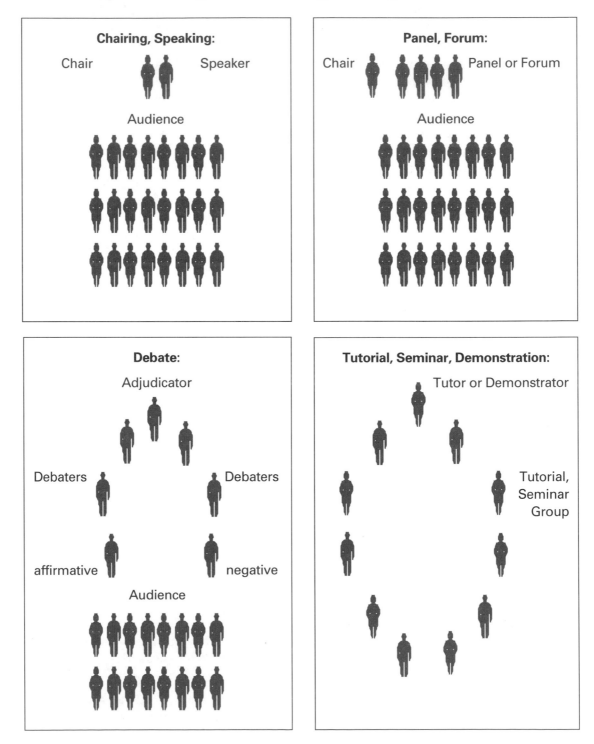

11 Meetings & committees

You might read in your local paper about an uproar at a meeting of the municipal council. In one council, one middle-aged member jumped up and grabbed another by the hair. Sometimes they shout abuse. Sometimes they walk out in a rage. So you can see why meetings have strict rules. There are often disagreements and people get upset. The rules help the Chair to control the meeting.

Meetings are called for two main reasons:
- to pass on information to a group, e.g. a residents' meeting to find out about changes to the street.
- to make decisions, e.g. a club meeting to decide on activities.

Whatever the reason, meetings need to be organised and orderly. Otherwise nobody gets heard and nothing is decided.

So rules have become accepted for managing meetings. The rules vary, but there are some that always apply.

General rules
- Every meeting must have a leader or Chair (chairperson, chairman, chairwoman), either appointed or elected.
- The Chair is given the power to control the meeting.
- The Chair must know the rules and see that they are followed.
- Members of the meeting must do what the Chair says.
- Decisions are generally made by a majority (more than half) of members.

There are two main types of meeting: public meetings, called for a particular occasion; meetings of established groups, held regularly. We will look at each in turn.

11.1 Public meetings: Airing an issue

Anyone can call a meeting, by simply putting up a notice giving the reason for the meeting, the date and time, and the place.

When everyone is assembled, whoever called the meeting may appoint themselves Chair, or a Chair may be elected from the group.

A public meeting: Airing an Issue.

Informal meeting

Work in groups of about six. Read the play 'Homework'.

The purpose of this play is to experience how a meeting works, so everyone needs to read the explanations in brackets. (The play itself is not very exciting, but it shows you how an informal meeting is conducted.)

A notice has been put up on the general noticeboard:

HOMEWORK!
If you feel strongly about this come to
a Public Meeting
at 1.00 p.m. on Monday, 1 March
in Room 40.

Homework

Cast: A, B, C, D, E, and F have come to the advertised meeting. They are sitting round a table.

A [*who called the meeting*]: Well, I think everyone who's likely to come is here. We should elect a Chair. Any nominations?

B: I nominate A.

A: I called the meeting, so I wouldn't be impartial. The Chair isn't meant to take sides. I think someone else should do it.

C: I nominate B.

D: I second that.

A: All those in favour? [A *takes charge until a Chair is elected, because* A *called the meeting. Everyone except* B *raises one hand*] B is elected Chair. Will you take the Chair, B?

B: I declare the meeting open. We need to take Minutes. [*Minutes are a record of the motions moved.*] Would someone act as Secretary?

E: I'll write the Minutes if you like.

B: Thanks, E. Is everyone happy with that? [*Everyone raises their hands*] We've come because we're worried about homework, aren't we? We need a Motion. [*A motion is a proposal which the meeting might want to support.*] Then we can discuss it and see if the meeting agrees with it.

C: I move that homework be abolished. [*As proposer of the motion,* C *can speak either now, or at the end of the debate or discussion. The advantage of speaking last is that other arguments can be answered.*]

B: Is there a seconder for that? [*A motion has to be put forward by two people, a Proposer and a Seconder. If no-one seconds it, the motion is not discussed because it would be lost when put to the vote.*]

A: I second that. I called this meeting because homework is just a shambles here. Teachers set it and hardly anyone does it. And then half the time teachers don't take it in. And then they don't hand it back for weeks. So why annoy students by setting it at all? [*As seconder,* A *has the right to speak to the motion and give views straight away.*]

B: E, as Secretary, could you read out the motion? [*The Secretary writes down only the motion and whether it is passed or not; the debate or discussion is not written down.*]

E: The motion is: 'That homework be abolished.' [*Raises a hand to catch the Chair's attention.*]

B: E, you have the floor [*i.e. the right to speak*]

D [*interrupting*]: That's ridiculous! You'd never …

B: D, you're out of order. E has the floor. [*To* D] You can speak next.

E: I oppose the motion. We have to do homework if we're going to learn anything. The

An informal
group meeting

teachers have to have something to mark so they can tell us how we're getting on. There isn't time in class to do all you've got to get done.

D: [*nods in D's direction, since* D *now has a right to speak.*]

D: I support what E says. By the time you get into the senior school, you have to do homework if you're going to get anywhere.

F [*raises hand*]: Can I suggest an amendment to the motion? I move that the word 'abolished' be changed to 'not be compulsory'. [*Any words in the original motion can be amended or changed. The meeting must agree to amendments.*] As half the class never does it anyway, it could just be optional. It could still be set for people who want to do it.

B: You have heard the amendment, 'That homework should not be compulsory.' I would like to say something. [*The Chair cannot join in the discussion without asking the meeting. If the majority agree, the Chair speaks. In this case,* A, C, *and* E *raise their hands, which is a majority.*] I should point out that a lot of people who do the homework now, wouldn't do it if they didn't have to. We are now voting on whether to accept the amendment to the original motion. E, could you read the original motion and the amendment?

E: The motion was: 'That homework should be abolished', now amended to: 'That homework should not be compulsory.'

B: All those in favour of the amendment. [D *raises a hand. The Chair doesn't have to ask who is against, if the result is obvious.*] The motion is lost, one vote to four. [*The Chair is not usually allowed to vote, but has a casting vote, which means that if equal numbers vote for and against the motion, the Chair's vote decides.*]

B: We now have the original motion, 'That homework be abolished.' C, as proposer, would you like to speak now? [*The person who puts the motion has the right to explain it first. Or they can speak at the end of the debate. But each person can speak only once.* C *has not spoken to the motion yet, and as the meeting is about to vote on it, the Chair asks* C *to speak.*]

C: I think homework should be abolished because we do all the work that's needed during the day. We work from nine to three-thirty and no-one can concentrate on thinking for longer than that. People need time for relaxation. They're too tired to take anything in at night, so you don't learn much by doing homework after dinner. So I think it should be abolished.

B: I will put the original motion. All those in favour of the original motion: 'That homework should be abolished.' [A *and* C *raise their hands.*] The motion is lost, two votes to four. Is there another motion?

[*The bell sounds for the end of lunchtime.*]

B: Our time's up so the meeting must be adjourned. [*If the meeting has to be stopped for some reason before it has finished, it is adjourned—which means it can continue later.*] However, as both the motions are lost we aren't likely to want to meet again, so I declare the meeting closed.

A: Well, that was a waste of time. Why did you all vote against both the suggestions? [*Now that the meeting is closed, the rules about discussion end, of course, and anyone can say what they like.*]

F: I know I wouldn't do homework if I didn't have to. You might want to do well, but there are too many distractions.

C: I proposed the motion, so I had to vote in favour of it. But I guess I knew we'd never get anywhere trying to abolish homework anyway.

F: What's everyone getting upset about? Nothing happens to you if you don't do it. You feel it nagging away, of course, spoiling your fun. Your parents keep saying, 'Have you got any homework to do?' but they don't stop you going out. And teachers ask you for it, but they give up in the end. So what's the worry? If you feel bad about not doing it, it's your problem. [*Notice that a lot of people have opinions in meetings but they don't say anything. They often have their say afterwards to others. The rules of a meeting prevent rambling comments like* F*'s because, though they may be true, they prolong the meeting and don't add to the discussion.*]

Running an informal meeting

The whole group suggests two, three or four topics for public meetings, depending on the size of the group. Write the topics on the chalkboard. The meetings are held in separate parts of the room. Everyone chooses which meeting they'll go to. The numbers will be uneven, since not all public meetings get support.

Each public meeting elects a Chair and a Secretary, using the methods in the play 'Homework'. Following the sequence in 'Homework', move a motion, second it, open discussion, and put the motion to the vote. The Secretary records the motion and how the voting went.

If one public meeting closes before the others, members can continue with informal discussion, as F did in 'Homework'.

The whole group comes together to discuss what happened. The Chairs can report the motions which were put up in their meetings, and how the voting went.

11.2 Committee meetings: Making decisions

Organisations like businesses, councils, associations, clubs and societies usually have a committee of management that meets regularly. Often sub-committees are formed to deal with particular areas. A football club might have sub-committees for finance, entertainment, and selection. Members of committees and sub-committees are selected from the members of the club, either for their special expertise or to represent interest groups.

A Chair of the committee is appointed or elected. The Secretary may be a member of the paid administrative staff, and not a club member. In social clubs, the Secretary is usually a member of the club because a small club can't afford to pay a secretary.

The Minutes are the official record of the committee's work. Club members can check them. Committee members must check them before the next meeting, and agree that they're correct before the Chair signs them.

An Agenda, which is an outline of everything to be discussed in the meeting, is usually sent to members beforehand. All members have the right to add items to the Agenda. A typical Agenda is shown here.

A typical agenda

The Coolinda Club
The 41st meeting will be held on Friday, 26th February 1995 in Carrobong Town Hall,
Room 3, Main Street, Carrabong, at 8.00 pm.
AGENDA

Apologies
Approval of the Agenda
1. **CONFIRMATION OF MINUTES**
   Minutes of the 40th Meeting held on 4th
   December 1994.
2. **MATTERS ARISING FROM PREVIOUS MINUTES**
   2.1 Consideration of venues for annual social evening.
   2.2 Treasurer's report on Club finances.
3. **ANNUAL SPORTS MEETING**
   3.1 Report from the sports sub–committee.

4. **MEETING DATES FOR 1994**
5. **PROPOSED NEW MEMBERS**
   Greta Kolowski, Sara McCroskey, Jim Smith,
   Hua Tong, Con Toulis.
6. **COMPLAINT FOR THE TOWN COUNCIL**
   6.1 Letter from the Lord Mayor.
   6.2 Chair's reply.
   6.3 Report of a telephone conversation.
   6.4 Letter from Ms. Mary Tomkins.
7. **ANY OTHER BUSINESS**
   (To be advised)

Bill Conway, Secretary.

Meetings cannot go ahead unless there's a Quorum, which is the smallest number of members agreed to in that group's rules (usually more than half the members). This rule prevents the Chair from calling a meeting when hardly anyone can come, in order to push through some decision that the members might object to.

Any suggestion or proposal put by a member to the committee is called a Motion. It is worded to begin with 'I propose that …', sometimes abbreviated to 'That'. This is because the Resolution or decision in the end will be in the form 'This committee resolves *that* $500 will be spent on refreshments.'

Any motion must be Seconded. This prevents time being wasted on a suggestion that only one person supports, and which will be voted against in the end. At least two people must be in favour; they are called the mover and the seconder.

Each motion or suggestion is debated or discussed. Every member of the committee has the right to speak once about the suggestion. The person who proposes it can speak once at the beginning of debate or at the end. This makes sure the meeting doesn't get held up in repetitive argument.

If any speaker goes on too long, the Chair can tell them that their time is up. Any other member can also say, 'A point of order. The speaker has had long enough to give an opinion'. The Chair may agree, or put it to the vote. In ordinary discussion, if someone talks too much, another person usually interrupts or tells them to keep quiet. In meetings this could lead to arguments, so the formal method is used.

The original motion can be amended or altered by a member of the committee (and a seconder), by changing one or more words or the whole wording, provided that it doesn't become a quite different suggestion.

Each motion must be put to the vote after debate is finished. An amendment is voted on first. If the amendment is passed, the original motion is ignored because it wouldn't be possible to agree to the original form as well as the new form. If the amendment is lost, then the original motion is put.

A motion is passed if a majority, or more than half the people there, agree and vote in favour of the motion. It is lost if more than half vote against.

The Chair has a casting vote. In the case where a vote is tied, with exactly half in favour and half against, the Chair makes a public vote according to their personal opinion. Otherwise, the Chair does not vote, because that vote would make no difference to the result; or, which is worse, it might tie the vote, and then there would be no result. This arrangement allows the committee to get its work done. For instance:

- Committee of 11: 5 vote for, 5 against: Chair votes in favour: motion passed.
- Committee of 10: 5 vote for, 4 against: Chair doesn't vote: motion passed. (If the Chair actually was against the motion and was allowed to vote, the vote would be tied, so there would be no result anyway.)

Meeting procedure

The Chair declares the meeting open if there's a Quorum.

Apologies are received and recorded by the Secretary. Members let the Secretary know if they can't come.

The Chair asks if the Minutes of the previous meeting can be 'taken as read'. Otherwise the Secretary reads them out. Someone moves that they be confirmed; this is seconded, and put to the vote. At this stage, any member can ask for corrections. Remember that the Secretary has made notes during the meeting and could make mistakes, so it's important for the meeting to check. If there's something from the last meeting that has to be followed up, it's discussed under Matters Arising from the Minutes, which is an item on the Agenda.

The Chair asks for the Agenda to be approved, and calls for any other items. Usually, members have to give notice, that is, tell the Secretary so that other members can see the item on the Agenda and be prepared. They may want to check facts, or prepare something to say in the debate.

The Chair introduces the first Item. The Chair may call for debate or discussion, and then ask for a motion to be put. Or a motion may be put first, and discussed afterwards.

The motion must be proposed by one member and seconded by another. These two have the first right to speak in the debate. They give reasons why they made the suggestion and try to persuade other members to vote for it. Others raise their hands or stand to speak. The Chair tells members when they can speak, and must allow them to speak in their turn.

The Chair cannot prevent anyone from speaking. But each person can speak only once. The Chair must stop them if they speak again, saying 'You are out of order.'

The Chair must also stop members who disrupt the meeting. There are set rules. Members must:

- not use objectionable words
- not use offensive words about another member
- not behave in a disorderly way
- not speak for too long
- obey the Chair's orders.

If a member disobeys these rules, the other members of the meeting may decide that the member

- must leave the meeting
- is suspended from attending several meetings
- should offer an apology
- must pay a fine.

Reports may be given to a meeting, either by the Chair or by other members. At the end of each Report, someone moves that the Report be accepted and this motion is seconded and voted on. Debate and motions may follow reports, of course.

When all the items on the Agenda have been discussed and voted on, the Chair ends the meeting by saying, 'I declare the meeting closed.'

Running a meeting

Work in groups of about six. Choose projects or events which the groups will be involved in. These may include:

- preparing for an event like a sausage sizzle or a cake stall to raise money for charity
- preparing for an excursion
- arranging a school dance
- working on a project which involves collecting a variety of material outside the school, interviews and so on
- a library project.

Each group forms into a committee, and elects a Chair and a Secretary. Ideas should be put forward for an Agenda. Anyone with an idea on how the task can be done writes it down and gives it to the Secretary. The Chair and the Secretary sort out the ideas and form them into an Agenda. The Committee now has a formal meeting and must follow the procedures correctly. By the end of the first meeting, the Committee should have a number of resolutions which have been proposed as motions and passed. The Committee must nominate people to do certain tasks. People can offer to do them, or others can nominate them. The Committee should make sure that everyone has a task, and is prepared to report progress at the next meeting. The Chair closes the meeting.

Now you all go away and do the task that the meeting gave you.

A week later, call another meeting. This time the Chair calls on each member to make a report. What action is suggested (in the form of motions) depends on the topic.

Points to remember

The purpose of this exercise is to practise committee procedures, so keep to the formal procedures.

If you really have to carry out the project or task, you may have to abandon the committee after a while.

In real committees, much of the work is carried on outside the formal meetings. Members get together informally to get things done. The formal meeting is used only to report on progress and get new ideas.

Everyone should take a turn at chairing a committee. Because the rules are so strict, chairing is not as difficult as it seems at first. The Chair must know the rules and keep to them, but should be polite and keep calm. Chairing is very good practice for public speaking.

Formal or casual?

People who are new to committee procedures may wonder why the meetings are so formal and use special language like Agenda, Minutes, Motions, Quorum and so on.

The answer is that, where members of a group feel strongly and disagree, any discussion has the potential to turn into an argument, and the argument into a fight.

The formal rules are designed to get things decided quickly and to avoid disagreements which delay the committee's work, and may even become violent.

As a result of long experience, almost every organisation uses some form of these rules, even if they treat them in a very relaxed way.

For instance, in some meetings, discussion is very casual, with people speaking about a point several times. This can work well, as long as no-one causes trouble. If a problem arises, the Chair can use the rules.

Even then, the Chair might use casual language, saying, 'I think you've made your point, George. Could you leave it there', instead of calling for a Point of Order, putting it to the vote, and forcing George to make an apology. George, if he has any sense, takes the hint.

12 Forums and panels

12.1 A panel of experts: Research and presentation

A forum or panel usually consists of three or four expert people who sit in front of the audience, and all give their views on one topic. The Chair introduces the topic and then introduces each speaker. Each person speaks in turn, and the Chair asks the audience at the end if they have any questions to ask the panel.

Variations

The panel may be any number of people from two to eight.

The Chair may introduce all the speakers at the beginning, and says nothing more until they've all spoken. Or the Chair may introduce each speaker as it's their turn to speak.

At the end, members of the audience can ask a question to one member of the panel by name. Or they can ask the panel as a whole, and the panel decides who answers. Sometimes questions are written down and collected, the Chair reads them out and decides which member of the panel will answer. This prevents long, irrelevant and unsuitable questions.

The first speaker on the panel can act as Chair as well. However, it's a good idea to have a Chair, since chairing a session is a useful skill to learn.

Panel

Work in groups of three or four. Each group takes a turn at being the panel.

Have only one panel each day, so that the audience doesn't get bored. If the panel is dealing with routine class work, however, the class or group could pay attention to three or four panels in one session, if there's time.

Preliminaries

Choose a Chair for each session. Otherwise the teacher or one panel member acts as Chair.

Decide how long each panel member will speak, say 2 minutes (total of 6–8 minutes) to begin with. A group may decide that one person will speak for longer and others need speak for only a short time. This should be only to begin with, as everyone needs to practise speaking.

Each group chooses a topic. You are the experts. You might choose a sport, information on cars, or a visit to Hawaii. Alternatively, all the groups could work on an area you are studying in class—a text, an issue, how to write an essay. What you say is then useful to the whole class, and if they're taking notes, they pay more attention.

Divide your topic into sections, so that each panel member researches their own area. This might take several days. You should work together and compare notes, to make sure you don't all say the same thing.

Writing the paper

State the topic clearly at the beginning, and explain which area you are focusing on.

Give your points in order, with numbers ('My first point', 'Secondly') or clear markers ('Next', 'On the other hand', 'Finally'). This helps your audience to keep track.

Introduce important points with phrases like, 'It is important to remember that …', 'You should notice that …', 'It isn't clear in the story whether …'. These phrases help your audience to note when an important point is coming.

Give illustrations or examples, and give facts. Illustrations, examples and facts are easier to listen to than generalisations. They help your audience to pay attention and to understand the point you're making.

Keep to the topic, and think about what will interest your audience. They want information that is useful, as well as interesting.

When you finish, use a summarising statement, or even a question: 'This should give you some idea how the engine works', or 'Having heard my account, would you still want to go to Surfers Paradise?' Don't say 'That's all', or 'Thank you' (the audience should thank you).

Reading or talking from notes

You can read your paper out, or use only notes. Practise reading your piece beforehand, clearly and not too quickly, so you don't stumble.

Visual aids

Panel members usually simply talk. For this exercise, don't bother with visual aids. Concentrate on getting your information over with words. (See Chapter 13, 'Demonstrations' for more on using visual aids.)

Note-taking

The audience needs to take notes, if this is part of a class study. This is a reason to speak clearly, not too fast, and to give points clearly.

Seating

Panel members sit at a table across the front of the room, facing their audience. The Chair sits either in the middle or at one end.

You can sit while you're presenting your paper, or stand if you prefer. Decide on this between you.

Introduction by the Chair or panel leader

Decide how the Chair will introduce the topic and the speakers. There are several methods, as outlined below. Make sure which one you are using, and write it into your speech so you don't forget.

- The Chair introduces the topic and all speakers: 'Our topic for today is "The Court Scene in *To Kill a Mockingbird*". The panel members are Tara, Anna, Han and Con.' The Chair looks towards each person as their name is given.

- The Chair introduces the topic and first speaker, and then introduces the other speakers as their turn comes: 'Our topic is American football. The first speaker is Tara who will talk on the history of the game.' When Tara has finished, the Chair says, 'Thank you, Tara. The second speaker is Anna who will talk on …'.

- The Chair introduces the topic and panel members (as above), but the first speaker (Tara) outlines the areas that all speakers are to deal with, so that the audience knows what's to come: 'I'll give an account of events leading up to the trial. Anna will describe what happened in the trial. Han will give the children's point of view. And Con will describe what happened after the trial.' Tara then reads her paper, or speaks from notes.

At the end of her paper, Tara may simply look at Anna, who begins. Or she says, 'Anna will describe what happened at the trial.' (The audience can be told twice: they often forget.)

Anna gives her paper, and introduces Han and his topic; he speaks, and then introduces Con and his topic.

When the last speaker has finished, the Chair takes over for questions.

Questions from the audience

Questions may be written or spoken:

- Written questions: The Chair says something like: 'Everyone in the audience should write one question on a piece of paper. The Chair will select some questions to ask.' Someone from the audience collects the questions. The Chair won't have time to read them all, so will pick out some at random.

- Spoken questions: The Chair says: 'Thank you, members of the panel. Are there any questions from the audience? Could you put your hand up and ask one person on the panel directly. Any questions?' (The Chair controls questions if more than one hand is raised at a time.)

Ending the panel

When there's no time for any more questions, the Chair says something like this: 'I'm afraid that's all we have time for. On behalf of everyone here, I'd like to thank the panel for their interesting papers.' The Chair leads the applause, and every member of the audience must clap the panel.

13 Demonstrations

13.1 Something to hide behind: And to hang on to

Do you sometimes feel as if you're under fire when you stand alone up the front of the class?

You feel safer behind a barrier of some sort. That's why speakers stand behind a lectern or a table. It isn't only to put their papers on. It's also to protect them from the audience.

People feel safer if they're holding something for security. Have you seen speakers grip the lectern, or the edge of the table, as if they'd collapse without it?

If you show an object, it's even better protection. The audience looks at the object and not at you. You don't feel so stared at.

Fortress table

You can do this with the whole class, or in two groups if the class is large. Otherwise it takes too long for everyone to have a turn.

Move the tables into a hollow square or circle. Put your chairs around the outside of the circle of tables, and sit down so that everyone faces the centre.

A box of small objects (toys, kitchen gadgets, office implements, tools, etc.) is passed round and each person takes one.

You each speak for 10–15 seconds, following the procedure below. The leader keeps time and as soon as they tap the table, you stop and the next speaker begins. Keep to the time limit, or this exercise takes too long.

Round 1: Sitting, with object

Each person, sitting, in turn describes their object, while holding it up and pointing to the parts being described.

Round 2: Standing, for the owner

Everyone stands up. You must invent someone who owns your object, saying how old this person is, what they look like, and what their personality is like.

Round 3: No barriers, for the origin

Now each person moves round in front of their table and sits on it, so that everyone is facing each other inside the circle. (You're no longer protected by the tables.) Remain sitting while you talk.

Put the object on the table beside you and don't touch it. (You no longer have the object to hold on to.)

Begin, 'This [*name of object*] was found …' and invent a place where the object came from.

Round 4: Standing alone, for preference

Finally, each person stands while speaking and sits on the table again as soon as they finish.

Hold your object quite still in one hand. Look at the audience, not the object, and say, 'I like [*or* don't like] this [*name of object*] because ...' and give your reason. You must try not to look at the object, or fiddle with it.

Discussion

Did you feel safer behind the table than in front of it? Or safer sitting rather than standing?

Did you feel safer doing what everyone else did —sitting when they sat, rather than being the only one standing while you spoke?

Did demonstrating the object make it easier to talk?

When talking about the object on the table, did you find it hard not to keep looking at it instead of at your audience?

When holding it in your hand in the last activity, did you find it hard not to look at the object and fiddle with it?

Did the audience find the object distracting or irritating? Did watching the object while the speaker talked about it make it easier to listen to the speaker?

13.2 Picture show: Demonstrations

Demonstration—
Pictures help both the
speaker and the audience

Pictures help both the speaker and the audience.
- If you're talking about something you can see, words come more easily.
- If your audience have something to watch, they pay more attention.

Photographs have a lot of information in them. When you look at a real scene, you unconsciously cut out all the unimportant things. Have you ever taken a photo of someone, and then found that there was a clothesline behind them, or a rubbish bin in the foreground? You didn't notice, because you concentrated on the person. The camera never lies, they say. (This is untrue, because clever photographers can make it lie with shadows and focus points.)

Portraits

Work in groups of four. Collect photographs of people from magazines and put them in a pile on the table. Take one picture each. Study the picture for a few minutes, looking for hints in the way the person is sitting or standing, lines on the face, facial expression, hair-style, clothes, background.

Hold the picture up so that everyone in the group can see it.

Begin, 'This person is called …', followed by something about the person's character and their background. Make up whatever you like.

Avoid saying, 'In this picture…', or 'I think …', or 'He would …'. Talk about the person as if they really exist. You are bringing the person to life as you talk.

More portraits

Work in groups of three. Only two of you have pictures. Each person describes their picture as above. The third person tells how these two people know each other. They might be married, or be brothers, or work together.

What you tell can be quite factual, just what's in the picture. This is an exercise in talking without preparing beforehand, not an exercise in creative story-telling. Of course, you can be as creative as you like. The emphasis is on talking fluently, without 'ums' and 'ers' or long silences. Keep looking at your picture to get ideas.

Going for a walk in a picture

Working in groups of three or four, this time use pictures of places. They can be buildings or country scenes.

Talk about your picture as if you had been inside it (past tense). If you have a picture of a country scene, you can start, 'I went down this road towards the farm house. It was spring. There were flowers in gardens, and two horses in the paddock …'.

Alternatively, talk as if you still are inside it (present tense). If you have a picture of a town, you can start, 'I'm in the main street. There's a shop on the corner that sells vegetables. I'm crossing over to the pub opposite …'.

13.3 Demonstrations: Showing how

Has anyone tried to explain to you how something works—just by talking? It's very hard to follow a complicated description unless you know a lot about it already. It's much easier if you can watch how things work, at the same time as someone is explaining it.

A science teacher demonstrates an experiment before students try it. A supervisor demonstrates how a machine works to a new worker. A craft worker or an art instructor shows a new skill to a group of hobbyists or young artists.

It's usually easier to watch how something is done than to follow written instructions. People who knit or make models sometimes get stuck, especially if the instructions use technical jargon.

One procedure for teaching a new skill is:
- tell me
- show me
- let me try it
- let me tell you
- show me again where I'm wrong.

You need to try things out yourself, though you can learn a lot by being shown and told. That's why this book is full of activities. No-one ever learned to speak confidently without actually practising, again and again.

A good demonstrator

To make your demonstration effective, you will need to:
- have the things being demonstrated

- have worked out the sequence in order
- have some wall-charts to emphasise sequences
- practise the talk which goes with demonstrating
- give examples of practical uses for this thing
- have the audience close enough to see
- talk loudly enough for the audience to hear
- go over main points after each stage or at the end.

Showing and doing

Work in pairs. The teacher supplies a selection of things which are used for various tasks, e.g. needle and thread; tin opener; bean slicer and other kitchen gadgets; pliers and other small tools; staplers and other office equipment; science equipment; make-up; calculator; etc.

Each person demonstrates one object to their partner. Take note of what you say, what gestures you use. At the end, your partner must carry out the procedure and tell you what you missed describing.

Your description might include:
- visual facts: height, colour, shape, material it's made of
- function of parts: what moves, how they fit together
- its use: what it's for and how it works
- its associations: history, the way it may change in future.

Showing only

Repeat this with groups of four or five, and then with the whole class in a circle, limiting each speaker to one minute. You should be used to demonstrating by the time you talk to the whole class.

In a class, there's no time for everyone to practise working the object, and the aim in this exercise is to talk fluently while you demonstrate. Everyone will probably know already how to use your object. You should try to keep talking while you show how the parts work.

Bringing your own

Work in pairs. You both bring some unusual object to class. You should practise talking about it alone beforehand. Be as clear and interesting as you can.

Again, this can be repeated in groups, or in the whole class. It is important to begin with pairs, so that people get practice and develop confidence.

Watch how demonstrations are done on television. Notice that the camera can miss out stages that take too long, like waiting for a cake to cook, and problems when the demonstrator can't make something work. You should be able to find demonstrations in cooking or gardening programs. Take note of how the demonstrators chat on, telling you what they're doing.

A live demonstration can't afford to have any part that takes too long. The audience would soon stop listening. If you have to show an unfinished and a finished product, bring two along.

Example: Testing blood-pressure

You will need a helper, a blood-pressure kit and wall-charts. They might show:
- what figures indicate high, normal and low blood-pressure
- what high blood-pressure is a sign of
- the stages in measuring blood-pressure in point form

- pictures of the equipment and how it is used.

You will need to research information on blood-pressure, and practise using the equipment.

Before beginning the demonstration, put up the wall-charts and place the test kit on a table. Place chairs for your helper and yourself. Leave sufficient space to move freely between your equipment, your helper and your wall-charts.

Begin with an introduction like this: 'One of the first things a doctor does when you visit the surgery is to take your blood-pressure. Everyone knows that high blood-pressure isn't a good thing. But not everyone knows how blood-pressure works. I'm going to show you how to take your blood-pressure …'.

Explain the equipment piece by piece, briefly.

Show how to take your helper's blood-pressure, explaining as you use the equipment and read the results. It's a good idea to talk to your helper, as well: 'Could you hold up your arm? … Your blood pressure is … so you're perfectly healthy on that score.' Make jokes if you can. This looks friendlier to the audience.

Explain the wall-charts, pointing to the section you are talking about, and reading out important parts while you explain them. Don't just stand there reading a chart aloud; talk about it as well.

Conclude by listing the blood-pressure equipment on sale for people to use at home. You could make some joke about people getting too anxious, and becoming malingerers and hypochondriacs.

You might finish by asking someone from the audience to come up and try taking your helper's blood-pressure, while you repeat the directions. Finish by asking the audience to applaud this person as they return to their seat.

Major event

You're ready now to give a demonstration to the whole class.

Prepare a broad topic. You'll need to research your topic, and you might have more than one thing to demonstrate.

Give some background history, some examples of how the object is used in other places, and some account of possible problems. Some personal anecdotes about using the object help to make the demonstration more interesting.

Here are some possible topics:
- how a camera works
- a science experiment
- putting a model together
- repairing a bicycle tube
- how to play Scrabble
- the contents of a handbag and their uses
- how a book is bound
- playing a musical instrument
- how a radio works
- collecting: stamps, shells, bottle tops, swap cards, etc.
- using simple carpentry tools
- the ideal sandwich.

Set up the table as you want it. Make sure everyone can see.

Have very clear notes for yourself, so you don't lose track. The objects that you're demonstrating will help to remind you where you are.

It's wisest to have only two demonstrations in each lesson, and then to get on with some other work. Apart from the time taken to set it up, the audience gets exhausted if they see too many at once. With this type of demonstration, they'll be watching and listening, not taking part.

14 Debates

14.1 Persuasion: Making a case

A debate is defined in the *Oxford Dictionary* as discussion (especially in Parliament), argument, contest, controversy, dissension, wrangling, dispute, strife or quarrelling.

Quite simply, debaters take sides in an argument and each tries to persuade the audience to agree with their view.

Formal debates have very complex rules. Here the rules are simplified so that you can practise.[1]

Why debate questions?

People disagree on all sorts of issues. Some people can be persuaded to change their minds, but we'll never get everyone to agree.

There are several ways a group can decide something that everyone must do:
- a majority vote wins (democracy)
- the most powerful people win (dictatorship or fascism)
- the group breaks up and everyone does what they like (anarchy).

Debating belongs to democracy, where each side tries to persuade people to agree with them, so they will get a majority vote.

In a debate, people can hear both sides of the question, and that helps them make up their minds. Some people are so rigid in their opinions that they won't listen to the other side. A debate at least helps the large group who are undecided or don't know.

Questions for debating

Work in pairs to discuss points for and against. Choose any one of the following issues.

Family
- whether to go to the beach or to a farm for the holidays
- whether a teenager can go to a party, or on a school tour to America
- whether money should be spent on a new television or a computer.

Local council
- whether speed humps should be put in residential streets
- whether rubbish should be collected once or twice a week
- whether councillors should have a dinner paid for by rates before meetings.

Parliament
- whether tax on cigarettes and alcohol should be raised
- whether speed limits should be lowered
- whether all refugees should be accepted as migrants
- whether euthanasia should be legalised
- whether abortion should be legalised.

1 Ideas from Lewis Knowles, *Encouraging Talk*, Methuen, London, 1983, are acknowledged. If you want the classic rules of debate, you should find a book which concentrates on debating.

Class group

- whether homework should be compulsory
- whether American school hours should be introduced (7.30 a.m.–1.30 p.m.)
- whether uniform should be worn by junior and senior students
- whether full-time education should be compulsory to age eighteen.

Each partner takes opposite sides on the topic. Even if you both agree, this is practice in working out what the other side would think, and perhaps in rethinking your own position. Take turns in giving your arguments. Note down the best points for each side.

The topics chosen by each pair can be collected and listed on the board. The most popular topic can be debated by a larger group in the next activity.

A small debate

Work in groups of four. You will practise debating without an audience.

Use a topic from the list above, or decide on a topic of your own. Here we will use the example 'Speed humps should be put in all residential streets'.

Two people will argue for each side of the question. It doesn't matter whether you agree or disagree. This is practice in finding reasons and presenting them.

In pairs, decide who will introduce the topic, and speak first; who will speak second and sum up. Work out your arguments, that is, the points you want to make.

Rejoin your group of four, and begin your debate. Using our example, it would go like this.

FIRST SPEAKER IN FAVOUR: I believe that speed humps should be put in all residential streets. They slow speeding drivers down. These drivers use the streets for short-cuts and don't live there. Children will be safer, and so will dogs and cats and people on bicycles.

FIRST SPEAKER AGAINST: Roads should be safe for cars, as well as people and dogs and cats—which shouldn't be on the streets anyway. Traffic humps can cause accidents to a car not expecting a bump. Car drivers pay registration fees and petrol tax and they have a right to smooth roads. The road belongs to everyone, not just the people living in that street.

SECOND SPEAKER IN FAVOUR: Traffic humps can be made of bricks or stone, with bushes and flowers, and become attractive gardens in the street. They can be safe places for pedestrians to cross. Lives are more important than speed, and drivers' lives are saved if they have to slow down. A car doesn't have to get damaged if the driver goes slowly. It serves them right if they're going too fast. Drivers don't obey speed limits unless they're made to, and anything that saves lives is worth trying, so we're in favour of speed humps.

SECOND SPEAKER AGAINST: Traffic humps may cause a driver's death if the car swerves, and they're dangerous to cyclists. Children should be trained not to go on roads anyway, and it's illegal to let dogs roam in the streets. Humps make a loud noise when cars go over them and wake residents at night. And who wants a garden in the middle of the road? So we're against speed humps as dangerous, noisy and ugly.

Small debate with Chair and judge

Work in groups of six or eight. Take a topic from the list on pages 104–5, or find one of your own.

Divide into sub-groups of three, half in favour and half against. Each sub-group puts together points for their side, and chooses two as speakers.

Return to your group. One non-speaker is Chair and introduces the topic and the speakers. The other non-speakers act as judge or a panel of judges, who keep notes of good points made. They confer for a minute or two after the speeches are over, and then deliver their verdict.

Follow this formal way of managing the debate. Uncontrolled arguments can get very heated. That is why debates must always keep to the conventional formula, and a Chair must be in charge. No-one is allowed to argue with the Chair.

Example

CHAIR: We are debating the question [*states topic*]. I call on the first speaker in favour.
FIRST SPEAKER IN FAVOUR: I believe that … [*gives argument*].
CHAIR: I call on the first speaker against.
FIRST SPEAKER AGAINST: I do not accept that … [*gives argument*].
CHAIR: I call on the second speaker in favour.
SECOND SPEAKER IN FAVOUR: In support of the idea that … [*gives argument*].
CHAIR: I call on the second speaker against.
SECOND SPEAKER AGAINST: Adding to what my partner said, I do not agree that …[*gives argument*].
CHAIR: I call on the judge [*or* panel of judges] to decide the winning side.
JUDGE or SPOKESPERSON for judges: I [*or* we] find that the motion … [*states topic*] is agreed [*if the side in favour wins*, *or* defeated *if the side against wins*].

Group inquiry

Work with the whole group.

Decide on a topic, using one from the list on pages 104–5 if you need to.

Make a list of people in the community who would feel strongly about this topic. Everyone chooses a character and gives their views, backed up by personal experiences or stories of what happened to them concerning the question.

Example

For the topic, 'Should speed humps be put in Fish Street?', the characters could include these:

- middle-aged motorist who uses this street as a short-cut to work
- P-plate driver with an old car in danger of falling to bits
- cyclist
- mother with young children living in the street
- retired resident with a dog
- teenager living in the street who owns a cat
- landscape expert called in to give an opinion
- traffic expert
- resident who sleeps badly
- a councillor.

As well, choose two secretaries, one to note arguments for speed humps, and one to note arguments against speed humps.

Each member of the group takes a role.

The inquiry is chaired by the councillor, who introduces the topic and asks each person to speak in turn.

Each speaker begins by saying who they are, e.g. 'I am a cyclist, and I often use Fish Street.'

The secretaries list the points for and against (try not to repeat points, even though different speakers will have some of the same arguments).

When everyone has spoken, the secretaries read out the points for and against.

The Chair then asks, 'All those in favour of speed humps please raise their hands.' The secretaries count the hands. This is repeated for 'All those against'. Everyone votes including anyone in the audience who has not spoken.

The Chair says, 'The decision of this inquiry is that …' and then says, 'The inquiry is closed.'

Semi-formal debate

Work with the whole group. This is closer to a formal debate, and may provide ideas for an essay on the issue.

Select a topic, and take a vote 'for', 'against' and 'undecided' from all group members.

Form into groups of four to discuss as many points as you can on either side.

Select two volunteer speakers from the whole group, one 'for' and one 'against'. These speakers sit at the front table with a Chair (or the teacher) who introduces the topic and the speakers.

The speaker 'for' speaks first, followed by the speaker 'against'. All members of the audience must keep notes of what the speakers say.

When the two speakers have finished, the Chair calls for questions. Alternatively, the Chair can ask whether there are any other points from the audience. Members of the audience raise their hand, and the Chair indicates who will speak. Speakers should state before they speak whether they are 'for' or 'against'.

Members of the audience note down any new points. These will form the basis for their essay, together with any material they research later on.

Writing

Write a balanced discussion on any topic you have discussed, using language and style suitable for each different type of writing:

- A journalist writes an article for the local paper, reporting the debate. The local paper wants exactly 250 words.
- The Chair writes a report focusing on the points in favour of the final judgement, not both sides.
- The secretary writes up the minutes, giving briefly the points made by both sides and the final decision.
- One member of the inquiry tells friends what happened.

15 Reports, seminars & tutorials

15.1 Making a report: Individual or group

When you report on something, you pass on the facts. You may be reporting what you did, or what you found out. The report can include comments and opinions, but information is the important part. When you report to an audience, they might want to ask questions at the end to get something clear. Or they might give their views on what you've reported.

A report gives information. In contrast, a forum offers views, and a seminar or tutorial expects the members of the group to have done some work on the topic and to join in discussion.

With a report, the audience just listens. If you're reporting to a committee, they'll want to use your information to make decisions. But no-one should interrupt before the end of your report.

Visuals

Make your report as clear and factual as possible. To assist understanding, you can use charts, graphs, maps, pictures, lists and tables. You can use an overhead projector, or wall-charts made with a felt pen on butchers' paper. The cheapest way is to write on the chalkboard, but this is difficult if you can't prepare the board ahead. You can't hold everyone up while you write on the board. If you're reporting to a committee, give them photocopied handouts of your report.

Planning

When you're talking, begin with a clear introduction. Include headings, numbered points, a summary of main points and a conclusion. These will help the audience to make notes.

Examples and statistics

Use examples to illustrate general points. Real-life examples help people to listen. Suppose you want to make a point about the lengthy wait for government housing. You could add an example to illustrate this: 'One migrant family with four children and a grandmother have been living in two rooms while they've been on the waiting list for four years.' Be sure to use typical examples; do not choose one isolated case to exaggerate the problem. Usually, reports give statistics instead: '427 families consisting of 2147 men, women and children have been on the waiting list for over four years; 726 families of 3007 people have been waiting three years …'.

When reporting, you should try to be accurate. You should also avoid creating a false impression by giving only half the facts. Leave that to newspaper and television reporters. A 'reporter' isn't at all the same as a person giving a serious 'report'.

Reports don't usually include jokes.

Reports given by more than one person

Divide the material between the presenters in a logical rather than a theatrical way. The aim is to provide information rather than entertainment.

Use visual and other aids to make information clear, and not as a gimmick. Reports are to be taken seriously.

Giving a report

You can begin by giving joint reports to the class, in pairs or in groups of three, or you can each give a separate report.

Selection of topics

Take topics from class projects, issues, or texts in any subject. Here are some examples:
- the theatre in Shakespeare's time
- how rock videos are made
- how slang becomes accepted speech
- what Greenpeace does and how it is run
- American programs on Australian TV
- the law on sexual harassment
- regulations on dogs by the local council.

Planning your report

This is an example of how you could plan a report to be given by three people. You've chosen the topic 'American programs on Australian TV.'

Divide the topic into three tasks:
- Research Australian broadcasting policy on American content, cost of programs, etc.
- List the number, type and age of American programs showing on TV this week.
- Write and use a questionnaire to find which programs (Australian, American, English, programs in other languages with sub-titles) the public (parents, students, neighbours, etc.) watch most often.

You might take one task each. Or you might work together on each task in turn.

Collect the information

The three of you will need up to four weeks to prepare your report. You might use tables, graphs and charts to show how much American TV there is, what factors influence its use, and how audiences react. You could make a copy of the program guide for one evening, with American programs highlighted. If your school has the equipment, you might even show some video clips of typical American programs.

The questionnaire

For this topic, the questionnaire could list the names of current American programs, with boxes for people to tick: 'I watched it', 'I like/don't like it', etc. Alternatively it could give statements like 'American programs are better than British or Australian for comedy/horror/soapies/news etc.' where people tick what they agree with. Or you could ask them to name their favourite program for the week.

You don't need to photocopy a questionnaire for each person you ask: that's too expensive. Take your own copy, and read them the questions. Provide enough space so you can add their ticks to the others you have.

Presentation of the report

Practise the presentation with all your visual aids, so that you get the timing right. The audience shouldn't have to sit through disorganised presentations, or ones that run out of time. The three of you should stand behind a table in front of the audience. One of you introduces the topic (as the Chair would normally do). One of you summarises your findings at the end.

Showing your visuals

When you show charts, graphs or tables on an overhead projector, give people time to read them. Point out the figures, etc. that they should note. Explain what the figures mean. Don't read the whole overhead aloud. But do explain.

Questions

The person who gave the summary can ask the audience if they have questions at the end. Any of you can answer.

Helping the audience to listen

The audience should take notes if the report is on a class study topic. Remember not to go too quickly if they have to take notes.

You could tell them there'll be a quiz at the end, and the prize is three Minties. Ask about ten questions on the facts in your talk. Make them easy, with short answers. The audience exchange their answers to mark them. Read out the answers. Ask who got everything right, and share out the Minties if there's more than one winner.

You could extend your research by giving the audience the questionnaire you used in collecting your material. Put it on the overhead projector, if it's possible, or use photocopies. The teacher might control handing them out, giving directions and collecting them. You could add the results to your report, if you have to hand in a written report as part of a work requirement.

15.2 Seminar presentations: A group of scholars

Originally, a seminar was a group of students who gathered for discussion under the guidance of a teacher. A 'seminarium' is a seed-plot, so you might say that the seeds of knowledge were being sown in a seminar. A tutorial was originally a session where one student was taught by a college tutor.

Seminars and tutorials have both come to mean any small class where an expert leads and the group discusses. In a lecture, the lecturer talks and the audience listens. They don't join in. But in a seminar or a tutorial, the whole group is meant to join in.

Usually one or more students are expected to present a paper, and the group discusses the paper, led by the teacher.

We'll take a seminar to mean a serious analysis and discussion of some topic. Here are some suggestions for giving a seminar.

If you're the presenter, you're teaching and leading the discussion. The topic will be something the class is studying. Some students might give papers to provide information on the topic.

You can just talk, or use handouts, questionnaires, overhead projections, posters, the chalkboard, or any object you need to demonstrate.

You can ask members of the group to join in discussion, to read something out, or to write something.

Members of the group are expected to interrupt you to ask questions, add points, or to disagree. But as presenter, you're in charge.

You can see that you have to be well prepared.

activity

Presenting a seminar

You need a group of about five to ten. The whole class is too big for a seminar.

Select the topic for your seminar. Here we will use the topic 'Reading your local newspaper'.

You are the main presenter. You can give the whole seminar, or you can ask two or three other people to deal with selected areas. You decide which areas, as this is your seminar. It's not a panel or a forum.

You'll need one to two weeks to prepare. All the members of a seminar group are expected to have done some preparation, perhaps just reading, as this is part of a class study. For instance, you could ask the group members to look at their local newspaper during this time, and list the types of information in it, or to bring a typical article or page.

Planning

Analyse one issue or several issues of your local newspaper. Decide on three or four headings for your seminar. Divide the newspaper into major sections (e.g. local news; sport; advertising), and deal with one each. Or take three themes: e.g. who finances and writes for the paper; what its content is; what its tone and political and social context are, that is, what sort of community it reflects.

Give facts to keep people interested: circulation (showing a map and figures); how big the paper is, number of pages; what percentage is photographs, news stories, advertising of different kinds—local shops, real estate, jobs, etc.

Illustrate what you say. Display photocopies of parts of the newspaper; charts written with felt pen on butchers' paper; handouts; and overhead transparencies. Don't provide the group with copies of the newspaper while you're talking: they'll begin to read them and won't listen to you.

Give the group something to do. You could bring a copy of a local newspaper and give each person one sheet (or one page). Give them headings: council news; personalities (children, old people, others); advertisements for shops, real estate, cars; sport; situations vacant, etc. They could make a note of their page numbers (e.g. pages 4–5) and list quickly what's on both sides of their page.

Let the seminar members take part. Ask them questions, like:

- What's the name of your local paper?
- How much does it cost?
- Is it delivered?
- Who owns it?
- How many pages does it have?
- What percentage is advertising?

Or you could ask opinion questions, like 'Is there too much advertising in the local paper?' You can give answers to the factual questions afterwards.

Another way of holding interest is to tell some sensational news items from the paper: the number of burglaries, what some of the reported crimes were, what local personalities have done (usually someone has reached their 100th birthday or there's been a scandal in the local council). Tell them some of the things advertised in the For Sale pages, or what jobs are going (usually babysitters, pizza deliveries, and some secretive employers who give only box numbers).

Give some of your personal views. Which part is most interesting? Is some of the reporting bad? Are some of the stories pointless? Are some of the advertisements sexist?

Have clear outlines. Always tell the group what you are about to discuss, e.g. advertising, local news, or distribution. Then they know what to listen for. This will keep their attention.

Sum up at the end with a general question: e.g. What's the value of the local paper? Is it mainly for advertisers? Does it help people to understand what their local council is doing? Would anyone read it if it wasn't free?

Procedure

Write out a clear plan of your presentation, with the section each is doing clearly labelled so that you don't have gaps. Put down when you will hand things out, when you will demonstrate something, when you will use the chalkboard.

Arrange the room so that the group sits round a large table, with the speakers at the head. Position the speakers so that they can use the chalkboard, overhead projector, etc.

Have all handouts, visual aids, etc. ready.

You can stand or sit. Some people prefer to stand because it holds the group's attention better. Others feel more comfortable if they're sitting.

In the beginning, introduce the subject. Say, after the group is seated, 'Could I have your attention, please', 'Would you please listen now', or 'We're going to begin.' Then say, 'The topic for this seminar is "Reading your local newspaper".'

It is a good idea to begin in a formal way. It seems friendlier to say, 'Okay, let's get started, shall we?', but you set the atmosphere for taking the seminar seriously if you begin seriously.

When you've finished, either have ready a neat final sentence on the topic, or it may be easier to say, 'That completes what we have to say', or 'That's about it.'

Points to remember

- Have clear headings for your audience to keep in mind.
- Provide interesting facts and your own views.
- Vary ways of presenting your information.
- Have questions for discussion and activities for the group.
- Leave time for group members' questions.
- Keep strictly to your time limit.

Suggestions for topics

- Some aspects of a text—novel, film, video, short story—that the group is studying. They should have read or seen the text beforehand.
- An author, film producer, composer, singer, actor: biography and their works. The group should know some of their work.
- A balanced view of an issue reported in the press and on television, followed over some time. The group should be warned to watch for the issue in the press and particularly on television—as the speaker will not be able to reproduce that.
- Any areas in subjects other than English, such as history, environmental science, and so on. The group should have done some preparation beforehand.

15.3 Tutorials: Small-scale teaching

Tutorials used to be like a coaching session, with one student and one teacher. Now a tutorial is a teacher discussing a topic with a small group.

In a tutorial, you should know something about the topic already. You should have read the book or article, seen the film or play under discussion. The tutor leads the discussion, raising points and asking questions. You must join in the discussion. The tutor does not give a talk or a lecture.

A tutorial is different from working in small groups in a class. In small group work, the class teacher decides what will be done in the group and the group itself is leaderless. But in a tutorial, the tutor is the leader and controls the group.

Essentials

Both the tutor and the tutorial group must be prepared. Everyone is responsible for doing preparation. Students should expect to learn as much from each other as from the tutor.

The tutor must encourage members of the group to speak, and maintain control of the discussion. As in a seminar, it's sometimes difficult for the tutor to keep control if the group are fellow students. As you're all learning to talk in public, the tutorial group should help the tutor. It'll be their turn to be tutor next.

The tutor and the tutorial group need to learn how to make the most of a tutorial. It's one of the best ways of revising and understanding what you're studying.

The tutorial group must:
- prepare work for the tutorial
- note questions they want to ask at the tutorial
- be ready to answer questions
- take part in the discussion
- help the tutor to lead the group

The tutor must:
- prepare for the tutorial in detail
- give members of the group any material well in advance
- make clear what members of the group should do with the material
- give a clear introduction, explaining what is to be covered
- make points clear by restating them: 'The first point is … the second point is …'
- raise questions and ask the group's opinion
- help every member to join in: 'What do you think, Mandy?'
- welcome every opinion, ask for evidence, ask for responses
- summarise the discussion at the end.

Leading or being a member of a tutorial is not easy. Even at university, some students don't prepare, and some are too shy to join in discussion. Some tutors talk all the time and don't encourage students to give their views. Some tutors don't prepare properly either.

Tutorials are invaluable and save a lot of time in studying alone. They work only if members of the group prepare in advance. You can't make sense of discussion of a text, let alone join in, if you haven't read it. You might learn something from listening to the others, but it won't make much sense if you haven't prepared.

It doesn't matter if members of the group know more than the tutor. This often happens. Even at university, you'd expect the best students to be better than some of the tutors. Since both students and tutor provide information and views in a tutorial, it's the combined result that's important.

Running a tutorial

Work as a whole class, then in groups of four to six.

Choose a text that's being studied in class. Decide how you will approach it. You could divide it into:
- sections: chapters or scenes
- topics: character, plot, setting, style
- characters: three or four main characters
- themes: gender, class, race, marriage, death, honesty, violence, parents.

Each group takes a different topic, according to the approach you have decided. For instance, each group could take one main character. Select one person in each group as tutor.

Preparation

During the next week, tutorial members study the text, and note points and questions on their topic.

The tutor prepares points, ideas and supporting facts to introduce the topic and raise questions.

Procedure

Each tutorial group sits round a table. The tutors give their views and raise questions.

The tutor can ask a member to read a short section to illustrate a point, and can ask a question of any student who hasn't been contributing.

Tutorial members must respond to the tutor, and raise their own questions. They must help, not try to compete with the tutor.

Jigsawing

Give tutorial members numbers 1 to 4 within their group. At the end of the discussion, all the people who have the number 1 go to one table; all the 2s are at the next table, and so on. At each table, there will be four people who have each discussed a different aspect of the topic. They listen to each other's views. The diagram shows how this would work for a discussion of the characters in a novel.

Activity 1   Tutorial (single characters)

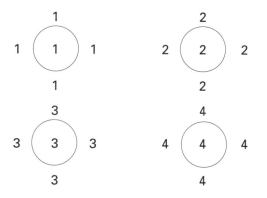

Activity 2   Jigsaw (how the characters relate)

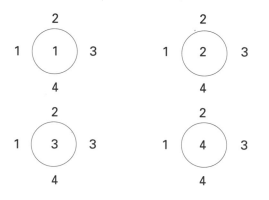

This is difficult to organise, and until group members are experienced in tutorial work, it's better if the class teacher manages this with the whole class.

Issues

Select an issue which is being studied in class.

Divide the issue into four or five topics, one for each tutorial group. For instance, if your chosen issue is 'Should Australia be giving aid to overseas countries when there are people in need here?', the topics might be:

- who is in need in Australia
- what countries need aid and what countries Australia is aiding now and how
- what Australia can afford
- what the moral issues are—advertising, appeals to emotion, charity, politics.

Divide the class into four or five groups and appoint a tutor for each group. Each group works on one topic. The tutors prepare material over two or three weeks.

Group members find what material they can on any aspect of the issue (any of the topics, not only their own), including noting television programs.

Tutors might give their groups some material or questions to consider two or three days before the tutorial (not essential).

Tutors prepare an outline:

- introduction of the issue
- some points to be made
- questions to discuss.

This should be in some detail so that the tutor has something to say if the group gets stuck.

Groups sit round tables with the tutor. Remember this is an exercise: group members must help the tutor to run the group.

The tutor begins: 'Our topic is ...' and gives a short introduction.

The tutor continues: 'There are a number of questions to discuss ...' and then raises the first question, giving what facts are necessary. Then the tutor asks, 'Could we have some opinions or points?' or 'Does anyone have any material on this?'

The tutor hands out a newspaper cutting. (This might have been handed out some days earlier. Members can share if any are lost.) The tutor says: 'What points are being made by this journalist?'

At the end, the tutor summarises the main points that the group have made.

Jigsawing again

Members of each group are given numbers 1–5 (including the tutor).

All Nos. 1 form one group, all Nos. 2 another, and so on. Each group has someone from each of the original tutorials who will know what was said on their topic.

In discussion, each group should be able to put together an overview of the issue which was discussed.

Keep this fairly brief, as it's a very difficult task. Group members haven't had time to take in all that happened in their original tutorial.

16 Technical equipment

16.1 Microphones, recorders: And the bathroom mirror

Listen to your own voice. How do you sound? One of the best ways to improve your voice is to listen to it on your own. You can practise speaking more loudly and clearly, more firmly, or more cheerfully and enthusiastically.

People judge you by what you say. They also decide what sort of person you are by the way you speak—whether you're forceful or gentle or whatever.

People also respond to the expression on your face and how you stand.

The bathroom mirror

When you're preparing a speech, take a good look at yourself in the mirror. Practise being more enthusiastic, more assertive, more polite, or more cheerful when you are by yourself. The mirror is your audience. Read your speech over and over, and watch your face. You may feel silly, but many good public speakers practise like this in front of a mirror.

Speaking and acting in front of a mirror

The tape recorder

Use an audio recorder to practise comments, jokes and speeches. Listen to yourself when you play them back. Repeat your piece several times. Listen to people you admire on television and try their methods of presentation. Keep your tapes, and after several weeks, compare the tapes and see if you have become more definite, more persuasive, more cheerful and encouraging. Act out being a good, confident speaker.

Microphones

Using a microphone is easy and yet many speakers are nervous of it. The class should practise with a mike. Often a microphone is a help, rather like a lectern, because it gives you something to hold on to, and to stand safely behind. It's also a mark of control and authority, so you feel in charge when you are using it.

For practice with a microphone, each person could:

- for the first time, give their name and address
- in the second round read a few lines
- in the third round say something they believe in, beginning, 'I believe …'.

Many of the exercises in the other sections can be used for microphone practice. But start in a small way. Don't use the microphone for the first time when you're giving a talk to the whole class, or making a speech. You need to practise how loudly to speak and how close to stand—and feel comfortable with it.

The video recorder

Being videoed is unnerving for nearly everyone at first, but people soon get used to it. It is invaluable to be able to see and hear yourself. Usually people are pleasantly surprised.

Practise in groups of three. If the class has only one recorder (which is likely), other groups should be doing other exercises and not watching. When the video is first played back, don't have the whole group viewing and commenting. The small group should see it on their own, and have a second chance so they can correct mistakes.

Filming in front of a large group can be done when people have got over their stage fright. For our purposes, this type of filming has no value, since most of the class will simply be sitting around watching.

Using plays and talks

Any of the plays in this book could be adapted for radio and recorded on tape. Playback allows you to improve speeches.

The plays could also be videoed, and several videos by the same group can be compared as performances improve.

Use of the microphone can be practised with any of the talks for whole groups in other chapters, especially panels and forums, reports and speeches.

If you're asked to prepare a part ahead of time, practise it in the bathroom mirror, or on tape. Then you'll be prepared for making a video. If you're making a speech of any sort, the bathroom mirror is there and costs nothing!

17 Small public speeches

17.1 Chairing a speech session: Introduction and thanks

If you're giving a speech, you can feel lonely up in front by yourself. That's why you have a Chair (chairperson, chairman, chairwoman) to keep you company. The Chair helps you to get started, and brings your speech to a tidy end.

If you're the Chair, you have a lot to do.

Before the session begins, find out what the speaker needs (whiteboard, microphone, etc.). Ensure that the room is set up, with chairs and tables in a suitable arrangement. Find out the topic of the speech and something about the speaker, so that you can make the introduction.

You and the speaker sit together at a table in front of the audience. When you are ready to begin, you rise, while the speaker stays seated.

When the audience is quiet, you introduce the speaker, and ask the audience to welcome them. You begin the applause. As you sit down, the speaker stands up.

You sit at the table during the speech and you must listen to the speech with interest. The audience is looking at you as well as the speaker, so you can't yawn or scratch or look around.

The speaker, having finished, will look at you. You stand up while the speaker sits down.

You look at the speaker and thank them briefly. If there are to be questions, you turn to the audience and ask for questions.

When someone raises their hand, you ask them to speak. If several people want to ask questions, you should keep a note of the order. (Sometimes the Chair leaves the speaker to deal with this.)

You decide when there have been enough questions. You can say, 'I don't think we have time for any more questions.' Then you thank the speaker again, and ask the audience to join in the thanks. You lead the applause. (The speaker never thanks the audience.)

The audience then applauds. You help the speaker collect their things, and leave the table.

Chair's introduction and thanks

activity

Work in pairs. A group of about eight students should be seated in a large circle, each with pencil and paper. No tables are needed. One of each pair is speaker, the other is the Chair. Decide on a speech topic and a biography for the speaker. Write out the first and last sentence of the speech.

When everyone has done this, each pair in turn performs for the whole circle.

Example

Chair and Speaker are seated side by side.

CHAIR [*standing, looking at the audience*]: We are fortunate today to have Bill Smith with us to speak about garden drainage. [CHAIR *looks at* SPEAKER] Bill has many years of experience in drains [CHAIR *looks back to audience*] and I know his information will be of interest to us all. Would you please welcome Bill Smith.

[CHAIR *begins the applause and while the audience joins in, the* CHAIR *sits down*]

SPEAKER [*standing, looking at* CHAIR]: Thank you, Alice. [*Looks at audience*] You may not find a Ninja Turtle in your garden drains but there are many other foreign bodies which may block them … [*Pause, indicating end of speech*] … And so I wish you safe drainage, free of roots, rats, leaves and floods. [*Glances at* CHAIR *and sits down*]

CHAIR [*rising, looking at* SPEAKER]: Thank you, Bill. [*Looks at audience*] Who would have thought that garden drains could be such an interesting topic? I'm afraid we have no time for questions. Will you join me in thanking Bill for his informative talk. [CHAIR *leads applause while sitting down*]

[*Audience applauds*]

17.2 Making a presentation: And saying thank you

People like to make a public occasion of giving a present or an award, to show their appreciation. It may be a farewell present, a prize or a presentation to mark an anniversary. The occasion is both formal and relaxed, and the more smoothly it's done, the less embarrassed people feel.

Presenting and accepting

The group sits in a circle and works in pairs.

Partners decide who will make a presentation and who will accept it. Work out what is to be presented and what the occasion is. Examples are someone leaving a job, winning a competition, retiring, getting married, or having a birthday.

Both people in the pair stand. The presenter and the recipient face each other.

Example

PRESENTER [*Holds the imaginary gift but does not hand it over yet. Looks at the audience*]: Mary Bullfinch has been with the firm for two years and as you know is going on a world tour. [*Looks at the recipient*] Mary, the office staff would like you to accept this portable clothes line as something to remember us by, and as a token of our affection.

[*Hands over the present with the left hand and holds out the right hand to shake*]

RECIPIENT [*Looking at the* PRESENTER, *taking present with left hand, shaking* PRESENTER'S *right hand briefly*]: Thank you, George. [*Looking at the audience*] Every time I hang out my washing, I'll think of you all. Thank you very much.

[*Both sit down. Audience applauds*]

17.3 Proposing a toast

You don't often have to propose a toast. But you may be asked to do so without warning. Or you might feel that a toast should be proposed, and no-one else seems to be doing it. So it's useful to know how.

The person who proposes the toast is usually called a Toastmaster, but here we prefer the form Toastmaker.

activity

Toastmaking

Make a group of about six in a circle, as if you're round a dining table. Make a pair with the person next to you. Each person works out a toast to their partner, using their name but inventing some reason for the toast such as a birthday, or a success. Or you could propose a toast to the whole family, for instance, or to celebrate a group success, in which case everyone drinks to everyone else.

Follow these examples.

Formal toast

TOASTMAKER [*standing*]: I now propose a toast to Helen on the occasion of her 21st birthday. Would you raise your glasses, please. [*Raises glass*] To Helen!
ALL, except HELEN who remains seated [*Stand, raise their glasses*]: To Helen! [*They drink*]
HELEN [*smiles, stays seated, murmurs*]: Thanks.
or [*rises when others have sat down, turns to* TOASTMAKER]: Thank you. [*Turns to rest of table*] And I would like to thank my family, my friends, and those who have organised this dinner. You have all been wonderful. [*Sits down*]

Informal toast

TOASTMAKER [*remains seated, raises glass*]: I think we ought to drink a toast to Helen on her birthday. Have you all got something in your glasses? To Helen!
ALL, except HELEN [*remaining seated, raising their glasses*]: To Helen!
HELEN [*smiles*]: Thanks, it's been a wonderful birthday.

17.4 Impromptu speeches: With audience help

Impromptu speeches.

Could you make a short speech if you were asked to, suddenly, without warning? If you were in a meeting, and someone said, 'Would you like to say a few words about the team's win?' or 'Could you make a few comments on that point?', would you be able to do it?

Some people like to be the centre of attention, and some people don't. But if you have to speak to a group—and most of us have to at some time—then this is one of the best exercises to help you overcome any fear you might have of an audience. An audience can help and support you; it can be on your side. An audience doesn't need to be frightening. Think of your friends in the audience, and speak to them. If it's a strange audience, imagine one is a special friend, and talk to that person.

You need to try this exercise again and again, so that you build up your confidence, and do better than last time.

If you keep trying, this method always works. After three or four tries, everyone can stand up and talk for 30 seconds—if they feel the audience is on their side.

It's most important for everyone in the group to help each other. Others in the group are very important in giving the speaker confidence. They can help by listening quietly, and responding with applause at the end. This makes a big difference to the speaker's feelings. You all need to make sure that there isn't anyone in the audience who's not helping the speaker. You should, as a group, make firm rules about talking, whispering or sniggering when someone is speaking. You need to be strict with those who don't join in the applause. Discuss the rules and agree on them, before you begin the speeches.

Rules for the audience

In small groups, work out a list of rules for the audience. These rules are to help the most nervous speakers. You aren't worrying about confident speakers at the moment.

Then bring each group's rules to the whole group, and work out a final list. Write it on the board, so that everyone can see it. You could appoint a Chair who makes sure that the members of the audience keep to the rules. Or you might prefer to leave this to the teacher.

Speeches made without preparation are called impromptu or extempore speeches. 'Impromptu' has the word 'prompt' in it, and 'tempore' means 'time'. Both terms mean 'without preparation', or 'on the spur of the moment'.

Look at the 'Essentials' at the end of the following activity. Then read right through the activity to the end. It's important that everyone is clear about the rules. You've reached the stage when you're practising for serious speech-making

Now you can begin the impromptu speeches.

Formal impromptu speeches

To practise regularly, have a few impromptu speeches at the beginning of each lesson. Speeches should be only 30 seconds long, so this should take no more than 5 to 10 minutes, especially once everyone is used to the activity.

Appoint a leader for each session, who prepares several topics before the class. Make the topics easy until people become good speakers. Topics can be taken from something the class is studying (e.g. character from a novel; an issue the class is discussing; something from science, woodwork, history, sport).

Appoint a time-keeper for each session. They will need a watch which shows seconds, and a bell, or they could just say, 'Time's up.'

The four or five speakers are randomly chosen, and not warned in advance. It's very important that no-one misses a turn. The leader needs to keep a list of the whole class which is ticked off as people speak, so the next day's leader knows who is left to speak.

The leader announces the first topic before naming the speaker, so everyone has to listen carefully. (Sometimes, everyone could be given a minute to make notes on the topics before the speakers for the day are chosen.)

The leader then names the speaker.

The speaker doesn't need to go to the front, but should stand and speak for 30 seconds, and then sit down. If the speaker can't think of anything to say, they should just stand up and then sit down. If the speaker runs out of things to say before the 30 seconds is up, they sit down.

The rest of the class must applaud, even if the speaker only stands up and sits down again. This is very important. The speaker is applauded for having the courage to stand up, even if they haven't said a word.

The topic

Here are some ways to choose topics. You could use a different method each day.

- Set a simple, general topic that everyone has something to say about: e.g. what I had for breakfast; what I last bought in a shop; my favourite food; my favourite piece of clothing; my favourite sport; something I wish I could do better; one of my relations.
- The leader or teacher lists a variety of topics on folded slips of paper and gives them out to the speakers for the day. No-one unfolds their paper until it's their turn to speak.
- Each person writes a topic on a slip of paper. The leader calls two names. The first person reads out their topic, and the second person speaks on that topic. Sometimes the leader can ask the first person to speak on their own topic. (This is a good way of stopping people from writing an impossible topic, because they know they might have to speak on it themselves.)
- Each speaker is given a letter, and can then choose their own word to speak about; you might be given *g* and decide to speak on 'gorillas'. Or the leader can name something beginning with the letter *a*, and the first speaker must use that word (e.g. *Australia, apple, arsenic, awful*) in a speech. The first speaker then gives a word beginning with *b* to the second speaker.
- Each speaker says something about a novel or film being studied by the class, describing either a character, or an event, or a setting. You could do this with any subject, or comment on an excursion or a project.

The speaker

The length of time to speak should be 30 seconds to begin with, and up to 1 minute when everyone is more experienced.

The time-keeper writes down the time when the speaker starts.

The speaker stands up, begins speaking, and stops only when the timer rings the bell or says, 'Time up.'

If the speaker runs out before the bell rings, they should quietly sit down without any apologies.

The audience claps each speaker. This is essential. Nervous speakers should be clapped enthusiastically, even if they simply stand up, say nothing, and sit down again.

The speaker should never apologise, or thank the audience. The audience is thanking the speaker by applauding.

The audience

The audience must listen quietly to each speaker.

Members of the audience mustn't read, or fiddle, or whisper, or giggle, or do anything to disturb or interrupt the speaker.

The audience must applaud each speaker, even if they only stand up and sit down.

Remember that you're going to have to speak, too, and you'll want the audience to help you.

Measuring your success

As you practise, you will achieve the following steps. Congratulate yourself for having:

- the courage to stand up in front of everyone else, even in silence
- the ability to say something, even for a few seconds
- the ability to speak until the bell rings
- the ability to round the speech off quickly before finishing
- the ability to speak coherently without preparation
- the ability to be witty or interesting.

If you can do any one of these, you have begun well.

Essentials

Observe these points for successful impromptu speeches.

- the speaker stands up
- the time-keeper keeps time
- the speaker speaks
- the audience listens quietly
- the audience applauds every speaker.

18 Making a speech

18.1 A polished performance: The final goal

You probably feel nervous before making a speech. The more often people speak, the less nervous they become. But how do you overcome nerves enough to start?

Some of the best speakers are always nervous: being nervous doesn't mean you are going to speak badly. Some people, of course, are not nervous at all, but they may be terrible speakers.

Some famous speakers and actors are quite shy people. Actors like Michael Caine and Laurence Olivier used their roles to hide their shyness. Nervous or shy speakers who are successful prepare well and set themselves certain goals.

In fact, it's often nervous people who carry out brave acts—in order to prove something to themselves and others. In the same way, shy people can learn to be confident speakers and prove to themselves and others that they are in control of their own lives.

If you've taken part in most of the activities in this book, you're obviously perfectly capable of making a speech.

The occasion
Speeches are made:
- socially: at formal dinners, at celebrations like weddings
- professionally: at conferences, at meetings, in law courts, in Parliament
- educationally: in universities, colleges and schools to pass on information, for assessment; and for speech competitions.

The topic may be set or chosen, and the language and tone has to fit the occasion.

Where speeches are made

List as many places as you can where speeches are made, and who makes them. You can include any occasion where one person speaks for a period of time to a group, and the group listens without interruption.

The audience
A particular audience will be in the mood for a particular kind of speech. They might expect to be entertained, to be informed, to be moved, or to make judgements. They expect to be amused at a wedding, moved at a funeral, informed at a lecture. For example, an audience that's come to a conference don't expect to have their time wasted with too many jokes.

Certainly, wherever they are, the audience expect to have their interest held. The audience's knowledge, age, and interests have to be taken into account. You won't talk in the same way to professionals, children, people in a retirement home and a group of your friends.

Audiences are very good at not listening. If they're bored, their thoughts wander and they switch off. They can't help it. So the language you use, and what you talk about, have to be right for the audience.

Types of audience

List all the types of audience you can think of. Include those where there's a wide age range (a wedding), as well as those where everyone is more or less the same age (a class listening to a teacher); and those where interests are much the same (a club), or very mixed (a theatre or concert).

The topic

Speakers have to take into account several things in choosing a topic:
- what the speaker knows well enough to speak on: you speak better on something you know a lot about
- what the audience's interests are: the audience listen better if they know something about the topic
- what suits the age of the audience: young children won't want to hear about politics, or old people about rock groups—though a good speaker could win the audience over
- what is appropriate for the audience: certain topics and language will offend or bore some audiences
- what can be covered within the time limit: too big a topic in a short time can be vague and therefore dull.

Fitting topic to audience

In pairs, make lists, two under each of the following headings. By thinking about topics which aren't suitable, you avoid making mistakes.
- topics I'm interested in finding out about; topics I'm not interested in
- what audience would be interested in these topics; what audience would not be interested
- what age group would these topics suit; what age group would they not suit
- who would these topics be appropriate for; who would they not be appropriate for

List also how much time would be needed for these topics.

Planning

It's easier to take in some information by listening, but some material is better read. There's a difference. If material is very concentrated, readers can go slowly and look back for points they have missed. Listeners have to take it all in the first time. You have to plan so that you help your audience to pay attention, and take in what you say.
- Plan an opening that stirs some feeling or interest and catches attention. For instance, on the topic 'Snakes', the opening 'Do you know how many poisonous snakes live near you?' appeals to fear; on 'The RSPCA', 'A thousand stray dogs have to be put down each year' appeals to pity. Alternatively, plan an opening which says clearly what your speech is about: 'I will be talking about poisonous snakes in Australia and how dangerous they really are.'
- Decide if you need overhead projections or charts to hold attention and make points clearer. Seeing as well as hearing helps the audience. For instance, you

could show a list of names of snakes, because people find it hard to take in a number of names without seeing them.

- Make sure you have enough main headings and that they are clearly distinguished as 'first, next' and so on. For instance, you could make points about the numbers of snakes, which are poisonous, where they live, how the poison works, whether snakes actively attack, antidotes.
- Use examples and details so that your listeners can hang on to some facts and can 'see' what you're talking about. People remember vivid details. For instance, you could tell stories about people who have been bitten, explain how one particular snake behaves, give visual descriptions for identifying some types.

Getting started

In pairs, choose a topic. (You can use the topic 'RSPCA stray dogs' for practice.) Write the following:
- two openings which will wake up your audience
- two charts or tables which may make points clearer
- some main points
- some anecdotes (stories) or examples which give a personal touch.

Preparation

Put time into this. Nervous speakers often don't prepare properly, and don't practise. Even preparing and practising by themselves makes them feel anxious. But if you don't prepare your material and practise speaking, you're pretty sure to give a poor speech. Knowing your material and hearing yourself speak (e.g. in front of a mirror) will actually give you more confidence. You must give yourself time to:
- gather enough *information* to hold the audience's interest: books, newspapers, businesses, other people.
- plan how you'll *arrange* it to make it easy to follow, both for you to keep track, and for your audience: show steps clearly, by saying 'first, second, my next point'.
- *practise* your talk out loud until you are fluent: talk to the mirror, parents, friends, into a tape recorder.
- make sure the *timing* is right, to avoid running out or going on too long: try your talk aloud with all your pauses and aids.

Writing the speech

Work in pairs, or alone. Take a speech topic, and make notes on it. Work out where you can find information; what words you will use to separate sections clearly; how and where you could practise; and how long your speech would be. These are only notes at this stage, and should not take long.

18.2 In front of the audience: Problems and solutions

There are many things that speakers worry about, or have to make up their minds about. Each speaker is different. You have to find out what makes you most comfortable in front of an audience.

One of the most important things is positive self-talk. You should think about practical things in your speech. Deal with worrying possibilities so you can be prepared. For instance, What if I lose my place? Answer: Mark the beginning of each section in red so you can see it quickly. Then put your worries out of your mind. If you expect your audience to be interested, they are more likely to be interested. If you expect to make a mess of it, well then!

Solving problems beforehand

In pairs, work out possible answers to all the following questions. Mark each question 'P' for a practical and positive question, and 'N' for a negative, pessimistic question.

These are genuine questions that all speakers ask themselves at some time, even when they're very experienced. When you face an audience for the first time, all sorts of unexpected things may happen to you. If you plan how to deal with them ahead of time, you have an advantage.

You may think it's better not to think about these problems at all. Nervous speakers sometimes refuse to face up to the idea of making a speech. So they don't prepare or practise, because they can't bear to think about anything to do with public speaking.

Two people may be equally nervous, and one gives a good speech and the other a terrible speech. The reason is always the same: the first has prepared and practised; the second has avoided anything to do with the speech until the last minute. You've got to plan ahead. (Some ideas for answers to these questions are on the following pages. But work out your own answers first.)

Starting and stopping
- How do you start?
- And how do you stop?

Questions
- Do you have to answer questions at the end?
- What if you don't know the answer?
- What if you can't hear the question?
- What if someone goes on and on?
- How do you end the question time?
- What if someone asks an insulting question?

Standing there
- Do you sit or stand?
- How do you stand?
- What do you do with your feet?
- Where will you stand?
- Do you get behind a table or lectern?
- Do you move about?
- What if your knees shake?

Hands
- What do you do with your papers, hold them or put them down?
- What do you do with your hands?
- Should you make gestures?
- What if your hands get sweaty?

- What if your hands shake?
- What if your hand shakes so much that you can't hold your paper?

Eyes
- Where do you look—what do you do with your eyes?
- Who or what do you look at—someone, everyone, the back wall, out the window, your paper?

Dress
- How will you dress?
- What if everyone thinks you look funny?
- What if some part of your clothing is undone?

Voice
- Who do you talk to—one person, front row, back row, everybody?
- How loudly should you speak?
- How do you speak into a microphone?
- What if the microphone won't work or makes a screaming noise?
- What happens if your voice goes hoarse?
- What happens if your mouth goes dry?
- What happens if you stutter?
- What if you mix up your words?

Audience
- How do you know if your audience is liking your speech?
- What do you do while they're applauding?
- How do you know if they aren't interested?
- What if they laugh?
- What if they start talking?
- Or yawning? Or going to sleep?
- Or get up and leave?
- Should you make jokes?
- What if they don't laugh at your jokes?
- What if everyone thought you were awful?

The written speech
- How much is written in full, how much in notes?
- How much can you read direct from your paper?
- Do you memorise all, part or none?
- What if you lose your place?
- What if you run out of things to say in the middle?
- What if you go over the time?
- What if you leave your notes at home?

Visual aids
- What if the overhead projector won't work?
- What if your butchers' paper wall-chart won't stick to the board?
- What if people can't see your charts?
- What if you leave your charts at home?

Disaster!

- What if you feel sick?
- What if you open your mouth and no words come?
- What if you run out of the room?
- What if you can't make yourself go into the room?
- What if you burst into tears?
- What if you faint?
- What if you drop down dead?

Now look at these solutions to the problems, and compare them with your own answers.

Starting and stopping

The Chair should introduce you and then say something like, 'I'll hand over to you.' Stand up, take a deep breath, and leap right in with a catchy first sentence. Alternatively, you can start quite simply with 'I'm going to talk today about ...' If the topic is a serious lecture, people looking for information sometimes prefer that style of opening.

If there's no Chair, you stand up, look at the audience until they're quiet, and start in. If they don't quieten down in about 20 seconds (which seems a long time if you're standing there), you can say something like, 'Can I have your attention please' or 'I think we can begin.' Use a normal voice first. Then use your loudest voice.

Stopping is easier. Try to have a neat final sentence. It could simply be, 'And that covers what I have to say about beach fishing.' Then you simply sit down, or look down and gather your papers together, or turn away from the audience to collect your things. In other words, you give a physical signal that you've finished and they can go.

If there is a Chair, you say your last sentence, look at the Chair and sit down. The Chair should stand up and thank you. The audience will applaud. After that you can start collecting your things.

Questions

Decide beforehand if you want questions at the end. If so, you must leave time for them. When you've given your final sentence, pause for a few seconds and say, 'Are there any questions?' Wait until someone raises a hand, and say to them, 'Yes?' If you can't hear the question, say, 'Would you say that again please?' or 'Please repeat that.'

If you don't know the answer, try to add something so that the questioner doesn't feel uncomfortable. Say, 'That's a good question, but it's a bit out of my area' or 'I'm sorry, but I really don't know the answer to that. Perhaps you could find out from ...'. Keep your answers brief. Don't start a new speech.

If the question is too long, say, 'I'll answer the first part. I don't think we have time for all of it.' If the questioner tries to start a discussion, you can say, 'Could we meet afterwards and talk about that? I think someone else is waiting for a turn.' Even if you're interested, the audience gets fed up with someone from the audience who goes on and on. You're the speaker, not the person from the audience.

If there's a Chair, they should ask for questions, indicate who can speak, and control the discussion.

If time is up and people are still trying to ask questions, say 'I'm afraid that's all we have time for. Thank you very much.' (Note that you are thanking the questioners for their contribution. You don't end your speech by saying 'Thank you,' because they should be thanking you.)

If someone asks an insulting question, like 'Why did you choose such a boring topic?', you have a choice of answers. You can answer seriously and thus defuse it: 'There's always someone to find any topic boring. I found this one interesting and hope some in the audience did, too'. Or make a joke of it: 'I guess it's not the topic that's boring; it's you who's bored, and I'm sorry about that.' Or by-pass it: 'I think I'll pass that one. Any other questions?' Keep calm, and don't answer with another insult (leave that to politicians); you might be outsmarted and embarrass the audience.

Standing there

Speakers usually stand behind a table or lectern. This gives them something to put their papers on. You can hold on to a lectern if you feel nervous, and the papers are close to your eyes. Some people prefer a table where they can spread their papers out. You feel more protected if you're behind something. For some speeches, the Chair will be sitting beside you at the table to introduce you and keep you company, and thank you at the end.

Nervous people often shuffle about on their feet. This is distracting for the audience, so try to stand still. Very confident speakers walk about, come round to the front of the table to emphasise points, and move across the front row to get close to the audience.

Shaking knees are a common sign of nervousness. The audience never notices, since they're looking at your face. Put one hand on the lectern or table for support. For your first public appearance, you could arrange to sit at the table. By the time you've taken part in panels and forums sitting down, you'll probably be experienced enough to cope with shaking knees.

Hands

It's odd that hands are so difficult to cope with when we're nervous; they look after themselves when we're not. Some speakers hold on to the lectern. Many speakers like to hold their papers when they speak, because that gives them something to do with their hands. But if your hands are shaking so much that you can hardly read your notes (and this can happen even to the most experienced speakers in a new situation), then put the papers on the lectern or table. Some people put their hands in their pockets, which is fine for a casual speech. You can hold a pencil or your glasses, but if you do, don't fiddle with them.

Gestures are important. They can attract the attention of the audience and emphasise your points, or they can be annoyingly distracting. Little fussy gestures worry the audience. Dramatic gestures are fine for politicians and salespeople but are irritating on other occasions. Some confident speakers have personal mannerisms which they don't even notice—scratching the head, pulling an ear, rubbing the nose, picking at a fingernail, fiddling with their glasses. These are harmless enough in conversation, but distracting to an audience. Rule: learn and practise some gestures which make you feel comfortable; avoid others; try to be natural.

Eyes

Where to look is a real problem to new speakers. Some catch the eye of a friend or a sympathetic teacher and talk to them. Some talk to a member of the audience who smiles or nods in agreement (this is very encouraging to a speaker). Some talk to the back wall, just above the heads of the audience. All these are fine.

Some speakers keep their eyes on their papers all the time. If you are reading your speech, look up sometimes, perhaps to emphasise a point or for a brief pause. If you don't, your audience finds it hard to keep on listening. You make them pay attention by catching their eyes. But unfortunately, when nervous speakers catch someone's eye, they often lose their place in the speech.

The ideal is to look at different sections of the audience throughout your speech, so that everyone in the audience feels included. It's common for good speakers to have one section they always talk to—the people on the right, or in the front row.

Dress

Of course everyone is looking at you when you're making a speech. But once they're listening, they get used to how you look.

There are all sorts of theories: navy blue gives you more authority; red catches people's attention; fawn or pale colours take the focus off you. People will make a quick judgement about the kind of person you are by your clothes and hair: are you conventional, smart, radical, to be taken seriously, likely to be amusing?

People worry that they might have a smudge on their nose, or a button undone, or tomato sauce on their shirt. The audience might notice for a moment, but they will forget once they're listening.

The answer is to wear what you're most comfortable in, as long as it is suitable to your audience. Make sure you've got all your fastenings done up and no tomato sauce down your front. You can ask a friend if you look okay. You have to get used to being looked at, and with practice, you do get used to it. Good speakers enjoy it. They like being at the front with everyone looking at them and listening to them.

Voice

You can select one person to talk to, though if you stare at them fixedly all the time they may get a bit uncomfortable. Whoever you're looking at, you're talking to.

You need to practise speaking loudly enough for the whole room to hear. One of the main reasons why audiences begin to fidget and mutter is because they can't hear easily. You need to go slowly enough, with enough pauses, so people can take in what you say. But do not speak too slowly. Vary the speed.

You should always practise with a microphone before using one. Find out how close to stand. If the microphone goes wrong, someone else ought to fix it for you. Stand back and let them. Don't keep talking into a crackling or screaming microphone, because your audience won't listen. You may have to abandon it and shout.

The glass of water is there for speakers who suffer from a hoarse voice or a dry mouth. Even in classroom speeches, have a glass of water there. Some people suck a sweet or throat lozenge before their turn to speak.

If you stutter or mix up your words, simply stop, apologise briefly to your audience, and start again. Many good speakers do this, and no-one minds. Often the audience laugh if you say a wrong word (a Freudian slip) by mistake, and all you need to do is smile and correct yourself. Very experienced speakers use such slips to make a witty comment, but that takes practice.

Audience

An audience has to learn how to be an audience, just as much as a speaker has to learn how to be a speaker. Bad audiences aren't usually the speaker's fault. That's why this book tells you about being an audience, a well as about being a speaker. People tend to judge whether they're a success by the length of the applause. But some people are very interested and still don't bother to clap at the end. It's quite hard to judge the success of your speech, so forget about it.

Some speakers don't feel they've got the audience on side until they get a laugh. Certainly it's a good feeling when the audience laugh. So should you make jokes? Yes, but not too many, and suit them to your audience. Practise them on someone else first, so you get the timing right. If the joke doesn't work, many comedians have a line they use, like, 'That didn't work did it?' or 'That was above your heads, was it?' But you need to be experienced to carry that off. If no-one laughs at your joke, just continue your speech. Often a joke which goes down very well with one group falls flat the next time you tell it. So don't worry.

If the audience laugh in the wrong places, just continue. If someone starts talking, you can look at them directly; or make a comment like, 'I seem to have some competition over there', or 'Would you like to ask a question?' For an inexperienced speaker, it's best to ignore them, since these comments can backfire and you need to be able to handle their answer, too!

If someone yawns or goes to sleep, you should assume they had a late night and that's not your problem. It's better not to make a comment. They might have sleeping sickness. They aren't causing you any trouble, anyway.

If someone gets up and leaves, assume they need to, and ignore them. If half the group gets up to leave, it's probably wise either to cut the speech short, or to say to the remaining audience, 'Would you like me to go on, or shall we call it a day?' (This does sometimes happen at conferences, when people want to go on to another session, or decide they've come to the wrong one, or are in a hurry to join the queue for lunch.)

It will never happen that everyone thinks you're awful. True, some won't be interested in your topic. Your method of delivery won't satisfy some. But an audience is full of different people, and they all react differently. You can't expect to please all the people all the time. Take notice of those who did like it.

The written speech

Write the speech out in full. Mark pauses. Read it aloud several times and alter sentences that are too long, too pompous, too slangy. Write it in the conversational language you intend to use.

Many people have the full speech with them when they speak. Mark key points in the speech in red, so that you can find your place easily. The red highlights what would otherwise be your notes. Practise thoroughly so that you can find your place after you've look up at your audience. If you lose your place completely, stay calm and look for it. You can even say to your audience, 'I'm sorry. I've lost my place. Ah, here we are', and continue. If you do continue in the wrong place, it isn't a disaster. Your audience may not even notice.

You can read your speech, unless rules in assessment or a competition prevent it. It's better to give a well-read speech than a rambling, stumbling speech from notes. If you know your topic well—if it's about something you work with, for instance—you may need only notes.

Memorising a speech is seldom a good idea. If you lose the thread, you are likely to be stuck completely. If you're nervous or distracted, you could forget it—however well you thought you knew it. But practise your speech several times, and some parts will stay in your head anyway.

If you run out of things to say in the middle, simply stop early. If you seem to be going over time, cut out a few paragraphs or points. (Put a green mark down the side of paragraphs that you could leave out if you have to.) Alternatively, you can summarise the last part, though this means you have to think on your feet; or you can simply say, 'Time is running out, so I think we will leave it here', and sit down.

Don't leave your speech at home! Check and recheck before you shut the front door. If by any chance you mislay your speech, sit down and rewrite it at least in outline. If you've practised well, you'll remember most of it when you begin to write. If you've really practised, you can give it from notes, so rewrite them.

Disaster!

You should never be expected to make a speech in front of an audience without having practised in a group. That's what the rest of this book is about. By the time you come to this chapter, none of these things are likely to happen to you anyway. But this is a new situation, all the same. You may be worried about some of these things.

Most of these disasters have happened to some speakers at some time. They are symptoms of stage-fright, communication anxiety or whatever you like to call it.

If you're nervous, have a friend come with you up to the last minute, right inside the door. Tell the Chair that you feel nervous. Sharing your feelings often stops stage-fright.

Take a slow breath, or a sip of water (but not both, or you'll have a coughing fit). Arrange to catch the eye of your friend in the audience (and tell them to smile and look positive!).

Have your speech written in full, so you can read it out if your mind goes blank.

Even if you feel slightly sick (a sinking feeling, butterflies), you are not likely to be sick. If you have your speech written out and have practised it, you won't burst into tears. You've got something to get on with, and that will take your mind off it.

Nobody I know has ever actually fainted while making a speech, let alone dropped dead. People with phobias think this will happen to them, but it never does.

18.3 Trial runs: Getting it right

Each stage of giving a speech should be practised, so you're familiar with the conventions. Throughout this book, you've practised these skills. Once you feel comfortable with them, you can make changes to suit yourself.

Preparing your final speech

Any audience has limited attention. Two speeches in one session is about as much as the normal audience can take in. So spread the speeches out over two or three weeks. If the speeches are on topics which form part of the curriculum, in English or other subjects, the audience will not be wasting their time. In fact, the speaker will save them time in research and study.

The only way to learn public speaking in front of an audience is to do it. You must now write your speech and present it to the group. You have had a great deal of practice already from the exercises so far.

Choose a topic, research it, and write your speech. You may want to use charts or overhead transparencies, so prepare them. Keep to your time limit.

Starting and stopping
Plan your opening and closing sentences to suit your topic.

Questions
Decide whether you will allow questions at the end.

Standing there
Practise your speech in the room where you will give it or at home, so that you feel comfortable about how you stand.

Hands
Work out what you will do with your hands. Practise any gestures and ask someone else how they look.

Eyes

Practise looking at a friend or one of the family while you speak. If you read your paper, look up regularly. Decide beforehand where you intend to look when you are actually speaking to the audience.

Dress

Decide what you'll wear—if you have a choice. Don't keep changing your mind. Wear what feels comfortable, and what you feel comfortable about others looking at. Remember, although the audience notices what you are wearing for the first minute, they get used to your appearance almost at once and don't notice it after that.

Voice

Go over your paper, reading aloud to yourself and then to anyone who will listen, until you're fluent. Most people change their voice a little when they're speaking in public (or even on the telephone).

Make sure that you can be heard; that you don't gabble (remember to pause sometimes); and that you don't hesitate and say a great many 'ums' and 'ers' (a few don't matter at all).

Audience

Check the tone of your speech. Decide whether a joke is appropriate. You don't have to be witty to keep an audience interested. Remember that your audience should be well trained to respond positively and helpfully, so expect them to be on your side.

The written speech

Have the full speech with you if you feel nervous. You can read it out, but try to talk without reading all of it, if you can. Mark headings so that if you do get lost, you can go back to reading. With more experience, you should try to speak from notes.

Disasters

The whole point of this book is to lead you step by step to this stage, so there won't be any disasters. Most of the disasters that public speakers have are in their own minds. The audience hardly notices, and if they do notice, they usually don't remember.

Critiques

After the speech in front of an audience, the speaker needs to get some feedback. You may think it's gone badly, when in fact it went very well. Or you may think it was quite good, but want to find out where you could improve.

Some groups use questionnaires that the audience can fill in, but looking at twenty sets of answers will probably only confuse you.

Generalisations aren't much help, like 'Use of hands: weak', or 'Opening: good'. Speakers need detailed information like 'Waved your hand round too much; couldn't concentrate on your speech', or 'Opening surprising; then you said what was coming. Liked that.'

One person in the audience could make notes on the good points and weak points of your speech, and discuss them with you afterwards. You should name the person who will write this critique. It is better not to have the person selected randomly or by someone else.

If you are asked to do a critique on someone's speech, list the good points first.

Under weak points, list only things that can be changed. Some things we can't help much, like our appearance or our voices. Only a few weak points need to be mentioned after each speech. It's depressing to get a huge list, and you aren't meant to be an expert yet.

As a speaker, keep a note of things that you might change next time. Also keep a note of parts that were good, so that you can do them again.

A model speech

The group leader or teacher demonstrates a short speech (perhaps including examples of what not to do), and every member of the group writes down the good and weak points.

Working as a whole class, list the points in two columns on the board. Discuss any disagreements, and whether the comments are helpful. Decide which comments should not be passed on to the speaker, and why.

Alternatively, work in groups of four to discuss how useful the critiques are to the speaker.

Final speech: Public speaking

Now, after many exercises and a full practice speech, you're ready to give your grand speech. Look back over the advice and hints in this chapter.

Your speech

Good luck!

Further reading

Theory

McCroskey, J. C. *Quiet Children and the Classroom Teacher*, ERIC/SCA, 1991.

Phillips, G. M. *Communication Incompetencies*: *A Theory of Training Oral Performance Behavior*, South Illinois University Press, 1991.

Talk and Learning 5–16: an in-service pack for oracy for teachers, Open University Press, 1991.

Practice: Classroom

Tarleton, R. *Learning and Talking: A practical guide to oracy across the curriculum*, Routledge, 1988.

Practice: Workplace

Heylin, Angela, *Putting it Across*, Michael Joseph, 1991.

Gender issues

Tannen, Deborah, *You Just Don't Understand: Men and Women in Conversation*, Ballantine Books, 1991.

Index

accepting a gift 119
activities, including
  drawing 4, 7, 9
  pictures 5, 64, 100-1
  writing 7, 8, 14, 41, 44, 49,
    57-8, 63-4, 65, 71-3, 97, 107,
    110, 112, 126, 128, 132
activities, group
  for pairs 2-5, 7-8, 11, 22-5, 27,
    30-4, 36, 39, 40, 42, 45-6,
    52-3, 58, 63-4, 66-7, 70, 76-
    7, 79, 80-2, 85, 102, 104,
    118-19, 125-6
  for 3-4 students 6, 12, 24-5, 27,
    30-1, 36, 39-40, 43, 48-52, 58,
    63, 69, 72-3, 77, 79, 82, 83-5,
    97, 100-2, 105, 113-14, 117
  for 5-8 students 10, 13, 27, 31,
    48, 60-2, 66-7, 71-3, 78, 90,
    95, 105, 111, 113, 115, 120
  whole class 5, 6, 10-11, 15, 18,
    33, 41, 44, 58, 60-1, 63, 66,
    68-9, 71-2, 92, 99-100, 102-3,
    106-7, 109, 113, 117, 119,
    121, 125
activities, outside 5, 6, 35, 37, 44,
    57-8, 65, 83
activities, solo see activities,
    outside; speeches
admitting ignorance 40, 85
agendas 93-5
aggression 41 2
anarchy 104
anecdotes, telling 66
apologising 37-41, 94
  accepting apologies 38
applause v, 88, 122-3, 131
arguing 55, 71 see also debating
assertiveness 41-2
audiences v, 87-8, 98, 102, 110,
    112, 119, 121-3, 124-7, 128,
    131-2, 134
Aussie Rules 15
autobiography 62

bathroom mirror 116
blaming 36-7
  accepting blame 42
blood-pressure demonstration
    102-3
body language 76
brainstorming 70-1
butchers' paper 108, 128

carpentry 63, 103
chalkboard 108, 110
charts 108, 128
chemistry 63
chorus work 17-20, 69-70, 73
closeness 47-8
committee meetings 92-5
communicating 3
complaints 36, 37
compliments 36

computer games 63
content areas 63, 97, 103, 109,
    110
control 26
conversation 2, 29-58
  fillers 35
  joining in 49-50, 52-3
  making 31, 82-3
  taking turns 52-5
cookery 63, 109
Coulmas, F. 38, 54
course interview 80
cultural differences 2, 5, 6, 11

Dahl, Roald 73
debates 88, 94, 104-7
decision-making 92
democracy 104
demonstrating 5, 6, 88, 99-103
describing 3, 4, 7, 8, 9, 63, 99-101
dictatorship 104
dictionary of slang 58
directions, giving 7, 8
disagreeing 42-3
disasters 129, 132, 134
dramatised examples 32, 49, 69-
    70, 74, 76-8, 81-2, 90-2, 105,
    117, 119
drawing 4, 7, 9
dress 5, 100, 128, 131, 134

Edmondson, W. J. 38
embarrassment 2
Encouraging Talk 104
examples, real-life 108
excluding others 45
experts 96
explaining 7, 63 see also
    demonstrating
eyes, looking 2, 3, 33-4, 61-2,
    128, 130, 134

facial expression 3, 100
family 104 see also groups, family
film, discussing 63, 71, 85, 112,
    122
first aid 63
football 15-17, 32
forums 64, 88, 96-8
Fraser, B. 38

gadgets, describing 7, 99, 102
gambits 53-4
games for public speaking 60-1
Gates, L. D. 15
gaze 3 see also eyes
gender 11, 14, 26, 30, 38-9, 40,
    45, 113, 136
geography 63
gestures 4, 5, 6-7, 21, 68, 102,
    127, 128
Goldilocks 73
graphs 108
Greenpeace 109
greetings 30

group behaviour 23, 31, 45, 47-9
  discussion 73
  leader 121-2
group activities
  for 3-4 students 6, 12, 24-5, 27,
    30-1, 36, 39-40, 43, 48-52, 58,
    63, 69, 72-3, 77, 79, 82, 83-5,
    97, 100-2, 105, 113-14, 117
  for 5-8 students 10, 13, 27, 31,
    48, 60-2, 66-7, 71-3, 78, 90,
    95, 105, 111, 113, 115, 120
  for whole classes 5, 6, 10-11, 15,
    18, 33, 41, 44, 58, 60-1, 63,
    66, 68-9, 71-2, 92, 99-100,
    102-3, 106-7, 109, 113, 117,
    119, 121, 125
groups, family 23-8
  school 24, 105
  workplace 24
guided tour 4, 64-5, 71-2

handouts 108, 110
hands 4, 5, 127, 130, 133
head movements 5, 6
hedges 35

ignorance, admitting 39
imagination 3, 4
impromptu speeches 120-3
inappropriate behaviour 5, 67, 94
interviews 39, 45, 75-84
  course 80
  front door 77
  job 81
  market research 77-8
  media 79
  panel 82
  street 76-7
  talkback show 78
  telephone 77-8
interviewee 79-83
interviewer 76-9, 83
interviewing outside 83-4
introductions 118-19
invitations 36, 46
issues, discussion of 71, 73, 89-92,
    97, 104-7, 109-10, 111,
    112, 115, 121
items on agenda 93

Jellie, D. 73
jigsaw discussion groups 114-15
job interview 81-2
joining in 50, 52
jokes, telling 65-7, 116, 124, 131
judging debates 105-6

Keller, E. 54
Knowles, L. 104

laughter 45, 65-6, 131
leadership 21-2 see also
    seminars; tutorials
learning facts 72
lectern 99

library project 95
listening v, 32, 52-3, 55-6, 62, 68, 110, 125
literature 63
local council 104, 106, 109

maps 8, 108
market research interview 77-8
'Mary Had a Little Lamb' 66
maths 63
media interview 79
meeting people 30-3
meeting procedure 92-5
meetings 89-95
    formal 92-5
    informal 90-2
microphones 116-17, 131
minutes of committee 92-5
mirroring 2, 126
misunderstandings 45, 51
motions, committee 93-5
mouth 2-3
music 63, 103, 109

negotiating 70
nerves 121, 124, 127, 129, 132-3
newspapers 73, 80, 111-12
non-verbal communication (NVC) 5, 6, 51, 76
note-taking 97, 108
novel discussion 63, 71, 113

objects 99-100, 102
observing 5, 6
opinions 54
outside activities 5, 6, 35, 37, 44, 57-8, 65, 83
overhead projector 108, 110, 128

pairs, activities for 2-5, 7-8, 11, 22-5, 27, 30-4, 36, 39, 40, 42, 45-6, 52-3, 58, 63-4, 66-7, 70, 76-7, 79, 80-2, 85, 102, 104, 118-19, 125-6
panels 82, 88, 96-8
parliament 104, 124
personal space 47-9
persuasion 104
photographs, using 100-1
physics 63
pictures, using 5, 64, 100-1
picturing 3
planning 109, 111, 125
play readings 12, 13, 15-17, 18-20, 117
plays Aussie Rules 15-17
    My House 12
    The Skateboard Terror 13
    Visitors 18-20
poems 66, 68, 70, 71, 73

points of order 95
politeness 26, 28
positive self-talk 127
posters 110
posture 6 see also standing
power 21-8, 37
practice 126
praise 36
preparation 113
presenting gifts 119
presenting information 6, 84, 100, 119
problem-solving 70-2
proposing a toast 119-20
public meetings 89
public speaking 87-135

questionnaires 100, 109, 134
questions 31, 84-5, 96, 98, 113, 127, 129-30, 133
quorum, for meetings 94

racism 5, 67, 113
references 22
refusing invitations 36-7
reporting 6, 57, 58, 63-4, 84, 94, 108-10
resolutions, in meetings 93
respect 26, 39
revision 86
role-playing 23, 27, 30, 37, 39, 47-9
roles 15, 26, 41-2
room arrangement 88, 98, 99, 112
rudeness 32

Sandburg, Carl 6
science experiment 103
secretary of committee 92
self-consciousness 3
seminars 88, 110-12
sex differences see gender
sexism 5, 26, 34, 51-2, 67, 109
Shakespearean theatre 109
shyness 32, 121, 124
sitting 22, 34, 99-100
slang 57-8, 109
snakes 125-6
sorry, saying 37-9
Soup 68
space, personal 47-8
speech critiques 134-5
speech timing 122
    model 135
    topics 122, 125
speeches 87-8, 124-135
    final preparations 133-4
    impromptu 120-3

memorising 132
    preparing 116, 126
speed humps 106-7
sport 63
stage-fright 133
standing 5, 22, 33, 61-2, 99-100, 122, 127, 130, 133
starting a speech 129, 133
statistics 108
stereotypes 28
stopping, ending a speech 129, 133
stories, discussing 63, 85, 112
    reading 85, 122
    telling 61, 65-6, 68-9, 71, 73
tables 99
tactfulness 43, 51
tag questions 35, 44
talkback show 78
tape recorder 83, 116, 126
teaching 5 see also seminars; tutorials
technical equipment 116-17
telephone 77-8
television 109
text study 63, 85, 97, 113-14
thanks 36, 118
thinking quickly 60-1
toastmaking 120
Toastmaster 120
touching 61-2
tutorials 88, 112-15

understanding 56

video recorder 117
visual aids 97, 108, 110, 112, 125, 128
voice 9-13, 60, 76, 128, 131, 134
    monotony 9
    pitch 6, 9
    tone 5, 9-13, 27, 66

wall-charts 103
weddings 124
whole class activities 5, 6, 10-11, 15, 18, 33, 41, 44, 58, 60-1, 63, 66, 68-9, 71-2, 92, 99-100, 102-3, 106-7, 109, 113, 117, 119, 121, 125
Wordsworth 70
workplace communication iv, 24-7, 51, 74, 79-82, 101, 108, 136
writing, included in activities 7, 8 14, 41, 44, 49, 57-8, 63-4, 65, 71, 72, 73, 97, 107, 109-10, 112, 126, 128, 132, 134